How to Earn
Over $50,000 a Year
At Home

Dan Ramsey

Parker Publishing Company, Inc.
West Nyack, New York

To my greatest fortune—
Jude

© 1979, *by*

PARKER PUBLISHING COMPANY,
INC.

West Nyack, N.Y.

Reward Edition . . . . . . September 1981

Library of Congress Cataloging in Publication Data

Ramsey, Dan
    How to earn over $50,000 a year at home.

    Includes index.
    1. Success. 2. Business. 3. Self-employed.
I. Title.

Printed in the United States of America

How This Book
Can Change
Your Life

You can be earning $50,000, $75,000, even $100,000 a year *and more* without leaving your comfortable office at home or the sundeck of your favorite vacation retreat. This book will show you how you can share wealth and prosperity with everyone around you by applying the dynamic power of PM—Profit Motivation.

Lean back in your chair for a moment and relax your mind; you're going on a pleasant trip into the future. You are going to see how your life will change with an income of $50,000 a year—nearly *$1,000 a week*. You and your family are enjoying your new, custom-built $100,000 home in a very exclusive neighborhood. Your month-long vacations are spent at your tranquil retreat overlooking the ocean, high in the mountains or on a far-off island.

Think for a minute about the palatial cars you can buy, without even having to ask the price. See yourself cruising along a placid bay in your gleaming sailboat filled with happy guests.

Imagine never having to worry again about money problems. Your biggest worry may be how you can spend it fast enough to keep it from the tax man. You can soon build up a fortune that will take generations to spend. And remember, many of these luxuries will be tax deductible, because you need them as part of your new and very profitable business at home.

It's not a dream, it's a prophecy. You can have everything you've ever wanted and much, much more by applying the simple principles you'll learn about in the following pages. These principles of wealth have been developed and mastered by some of the world's richest men. You'll learn about the value of **GOLD**, Dollar Dynamics, the Fail-Safe System to riches, the Two-Pocket Formula, your Wealth Worksheet, Selling Dynamics and more.

Best of all, you'll be able to apply these profit principles today—right now—as you read them. And, you can begin your search for riches with little or none of your own dollars, and without risking your current job or taking hours away from your family and friends.

My profession brings me in contact with hundreds of successful businessmen each week, and many of them have willingly shared their secrets of wealth and prosperity with me. I've also operated my own profitable businesses and learned many things the hard way before I found out how *easy* the easy way really is. In the coming pages, I'll share these stories of success with you. I'll give you facts and ideas, any one of which may give you all of the wealth and happiness you've searched a lifetime for.

You, my friend, have the right and the power to be as rich and successful as you want. An income of $50,000 a year is just a small start on your road to prosperity. In fact, if I told you now how much some of the people using these principles of Profit Motivation are making each year, you might not believe me.

You'll believe me when it's you who is making the money.

So, take a deep breath, lean back and turn the page into the rest of your life.

Dan Ramsey

The people who get on in this world
are the people who get up and look
for the circumstances they want, and,
if they can't find them, make them.

—George Bernard Shaw

Contents

1

Finding Your Future With the Power of PM

You have the power within you right now to earn over $50,000 a year from your own home or any other place you choose. It's the Power of Profit Motivation.

The Power will open your mind and your life to new ideas—ideas that can take you from where you are today to a new world of wealth and prosperity beyond your dreams.

Learn about this power. Use it. Make it a part of your life and you can reach *any* goal you set for yourself—including the goal of fabulous wealth.

HOW BILL M. SOLD HIS WAY TO WEALTH

Bill M. used to install telephones. Three years ago, at the age of 41, Bill decided that the best way to develop his personal wealth plan was to begin selling a high-priced item at a profitable commission. The only problem was that Bill disliked sales work.

A friend told Bill about selling homes for other people; he could earn $1,500 to $3,000 on the listing and sale of an average home. Bill quickly figured out that if he could sell only one home a month, he could make a living nearly twice as prosperous as his current job. And, Bill told himself, people would come to him to buy a home—with no high-pressure sales. He liked helping people.

Today, Bill operates his own real estate brokerage firm from his home. He began with $200 of his own money for supplies and the first few ads in the newspaper. That small investment has grown into a lucrative business that brings Bill over $50,000 income a year. That was Bill's goal. He earns it with income from his rental homes plus the commission he receives by maintaining his business goal of listing and selling two homes a month. Sometimes, it takes Bill three or four weeks to reach his monthly goal, but Bill often achieves his goal by the end of the second week of the month. Then, he takes off until the beginning of the next month to fish, travel or just plain enjoy his family. Bill knows he could easily earn $100,000 a year if he set his mind to it, but $50,000 a year does him just fine and gives him the opportunity to enjoy some of the wealth he's earned through the Power of Profit Motivation.

OPEN YOUR MIND TO A WORLD OF WEALTH

Just what is this so-called Profit Motivation? Profit is surplus money earned through the use of other money or labor; motivation is an incentive, an inducement, or a reason for someone—including yourself—to do something. Self-motivation is giving yourself a reason to reach a chosen goal. So—

Profit Motivation is the ambition for personal wealth strong enough to move you to do what is necessary to gain it.

Profit Motivation is the drive for riches that uses the leverage of time, talent and money. It is the incentive to create opportunities for wealth and then capitalize on them.

Profit Motivation is used every day by thousands of people who are looking for financial wealth, but only a few of these thousands know the real Power of Profit Motivation. The *Power* is more. The Power not only helps you set your own goals, but—more important—works within you and others to help you reach those goals. The Power has taken over in the lives of thousands of people in the last two centuries to bring them wealth and happiness as they had never known before.

The Power of Profit Motivation is the power of the conscious and subconscious minds to clarify and act on well-defined problems and goals because they have been motivated to do so with a positive end result.

The Power is strong and forceful. The Power can work within you each and every hour to bring solutions to problems that stand between you and your clearly defined goals. The Power is within you right now to use as you wish. The Power can help you reach your goal of $50,000, $75,000, even $100,000 a year or move you to attain a total financial worth of $1,000,000 or more. The Power is yours.

BUILD YOUR OWN ROAD TO RICHES WITH THE POWER OF PM

This entire chapter shows how you can bring wealth and happiness to your own life with the Power of Profit

Motivation. To fully understand the Power, let's take it apart to see how it works and how it can be applied to *your* life.

Disassembled, the Power of Profit Motivation is made up of these steps:

- Define your goal or problem clearly.
- Motivate yourself toward that goal.
- List methods of reaching your goal.
- Outline your short-range goals.
- Meditate on the problem.
- Be prepared for the solution.

Plan Your Wealth Destination

The first step to using the Power of PM is to define your own life's goals. What do you really want from this existence? *Happiness.* But what kind of happiness? And how can you find it?

That's the first problem you'll want to solve with your new-found Power: how are you going to find happiness in this life? Think about it for a moment.

This is a world of exchange; you exchange something you have for something you want. If you want happiness, you are going to have to give something for it. So what you want is an abundance of property that you can readily exchange for things that make you happy. An abundance of property: wealth. So, wealth—responsible wealth—*can* bring you happiness.

Is this answer to your problem of finding happiness correct? Can wealth really bring you happiness? Let's look at it further.

Self-earned wealth not only brings you the material things for a comfortable life, but also offers you reason for self-respect and the love and respect of others. Wealth also allows you to give surplus riches to others and offer happiness to them. It gives you a comfortable life, self-respect and the respect of others. Those terms sound like a solid definition of happiness.

You should now realize that your prime interest in life is finding and giving happiness and that you can readily exchange wealth for happiness. Now, you are going to set your life's financial goal so that you can enjoy the wealth and happiness you are searching for.

What is your specific wealth goal—$30,000 a year? $50,000? $100,000? or a lump sum like $1,000,000?

Only a small percentage of the population of this capitalistic nation earn over $50,000 a year. Usually, only the highly educated or highly ambitious make it to this plateau and beyond. $50,000 a year is about $1,000 a week. $50,000 a year means living in a home worth over $100,000. People who make over $50,000 a year usually own at least two expensive cars, travel extensively and move in nearly any circle they wish. Quite often, a person earning over $50,000 a year has a second home, a retreat, at the ocean, in the mountains or at a popular resort. An income of over $50,000 a year offers you a piece of "the good life."

Earning over $50,000 a year will not let you buy *anything* you want, but it will open up a new world of luxuries and offer you the opportunity to help others through charitable donations, scholarships and gifts. Even as you spend your impressive, self-earned salary you will be making jobs for others and giving them opportunities for wealth.

So, $50,000 a year is an impressive—but realistic—goal to begin with. Later, as you see the strength you have with the Power of PM, you'll want to raise your goals upwards to $100,000 and more. For right now, set your financial goal at $50,000 a year and you have taken the biggest step toward reaching it.

Bring Your Wealth Home

The second part of defining your goal is deciding the conditions of earning your fortune, because you want to enjoy making it. You want to be able to earn your fortune in a pleasing environment during your chosen work hours. You want more than just money; you want freedom.

Thousands of wealthy and enterprising people never have to leave the comfort of their own home or vacation retreat to earn riches. No traffic jams or parking meters for them. They build their fortune the smart way—at home. They can work mornings or evenings, take any days off they wish, enjoy meals and breaks with their family and still earn *four times* what the average American earns.

You have taken the first step toward your well-paying future with the Power of Profit Motivation. Step one of the Power of PM has offered you your goal: to earn over $50,000 income a year at home. You can, with the Power of Profit Motivation and the principles of success offered in these 12 chapters, earn $50,000 and more from nearly any place you choose. The Power is yours.

See Yourself Succeed

Money has no value—until it is used. The wealthy who don't use their money to improve their lives are really very poor. Look at your own plans for your wealth goal. How would your life change if you started earning $50,000 a year today? What would you do with it? What would you buy? A new house? New cars? A motor home? A trip to Europe?

Byron A. set his personal wealth goal at $60,000, to be achieved within six years. Then, he tried to visualize exactly how reaching his goal would improve his life. He even went a step further, wrote a $60,000 check (less estimated taxes) to himself, and started listing the ways he would spend it in the following year.

Byron first listed his normal overhead expenses, but they took only a third of his check. So, he started writing down the things he *wanted* to spend his new wealth on. He came up with a fully equipped ski boat and water-skiing lessons at a nearby resort, special furnishings for his new coastal home, an education fund for his seven-year old son, an investment fund for his retirement, the newest model of his favorite car (with all the extras) and a healthy donation to a local boys' club in which he had been a member as a child.

Then, Byron sat back in a comfortable chair and visualized himself learning to water-ski, driving his new car cross-country, enjoying the furnishings of his cabin at the coast and watching his son succeed in college. Byron *saw himself* succeed. He watched himself spending the money he was going to earn through the Power of Profit Motivation.

You can do the same. Start spending your new wealth in your mind right now. See yourself reaching your own financial goal and using it to enrich your life. Write yourself a check, and list the ways you plan to spend it. In other words, *motivate yourself* with clearly defined results you can expect when you reach your chosen goal. It's part of the Power of Profit Motivation.

Plan Your Way to Wealth

There are at least a dozen ways of reaching nearly any destination in the world. The right one for you depends on where you are right now—and where you want to go.

Our friend, Byron A., saw many roads to his destination of $60,000 a year within six years. He considered a woodworking shop, a welding shop, investing in antiques, opening a campground or mobile home park, making cabinets and a number of other profitable trades and businesses which he had skills for. The road Byron finally chose combined a number of his skills with his interest in camping. With just $75 of his own money and his home workshop,

Byron started making camper canopies in his garage. Within weeks, Byron was supplying a local truck dealership with a canopy for every new pick-up they sold. Their business boomed, Byron's business boomed and Byron was on his road to wealth.

How will you reach your goal? What kind of profitable ventures are you qualified for? What skills could you capitalize on? What are the possibilities available to you on your road to riches?

It's list-time again. Make a list of the ways you would *like* to earn your fortune. Not just the ways you *could* earn your wealth, but a larger list of ways you would also *enjoy* earning it. Don't worry about how practical they are just yet. The Power of PM will work on that for you.

Mark Your Roadmap to Riches

You can see your destination and can visualize what you will do when you get there. You know the different roads that can take you there. It's time to plan your trip by planning short trips.

No one ever becomes a millionaire—unless they first become a half-millionaire, a hundred-thousandaire, a thousandaire and a hundredaire. That is the way you'll plan your goal. If your own goal is $50,000 a year in income, you'll first have to earn $40,000, $30,000, $20,000 a year and so on.

Here's a way to bridge that gap. Write down your current income, then write down your goal. Is there a large gap? Divide the difference in half, then half again, then once more. The gap isn't as wide now because there is a ladder across it and you only have to take it a rung at a time.

Back to Byron A. When Byron set his $60,000/6 year goal, he was only earning about $7,500 a year, and the gap between the two was tremendous. But, Byron figured that if he doubled his income three times—$15,000, $30,000, then

$60,000—he would reach his goal. Byron wanted to reach his goal in six years, so his natural short-range financial goals were to double his income every two years, which made it appear much more attainable. So, Byron's first goal wasn't to earn $60,000 a year in six years, but he intended to reach his shorter range goal of earning $15,000 a year in two years. Driven by the Power of Profit Motivation, Byron easily reached his short-range goal on time.

Plan your own trip toward your long-range goal the same way. Break it down into short-range goals with definite dates for completion and, before you know it, you will be enjoying the wealth and prosperity of your long-range goal and looking for an even larger one.

Let the Power of PM Take Over

Science, in all its modern wisdom, knows more about outer space than it does about the "inner space," the human mind. They know what it is made of, how many cells it has and how the simpler thought processes work, but scientists still don't know much about the brain's subconscious powers. They have seen the power of the mind in countless tests, but they cannot explain how it can repeatedly have knowledge of things that have not been fed to it through the conscious mind. Extra sensory perception (ESP) is just one small example—the tip of the iceberg—of the power of the mind. Experiments have shown that, rather than knowing more about the human mind, scientists know relatively less about it than they did a decade ago.

The principle of electricity is based on theory, yet it doesn't stop any of us from plugging into the socket and using the power in nearly everything we do. Even without a full understanding of the workings of the mind, we can use the theories we have and the principles we've proven to command some of the complex power locked inside each of us.

The Power of Profit Motivation can be used in your own life to build wealth beyond your current reality. Believe in the Power and you can soon be on the road to realizing a lifetime of dreams. Unlock the Power of Profit Motivation within you *right now* by following these steps:

• **Find a quiet room, sit down in a comfortable chair and completely relax. Turn the lights out or hum a note to yourself to help you blank everything from your mind.**

• **Remind yourself of the value of your goal—to earn at least $50,000 a year from your own home or any other place you choose. Think about the happiness you can bring to yourself, your family and friends through the responsible use of the wealth you are about to earn.**

• **Tell yourself, "I have the Power within me to earn riches and find happiness greater than my dreams." Say it again. And again. Write it down on a small card and carry it with you in your pocket or purse. Remind yourself of this Power every day by rereading your note to yourself. You have the Power to make it true.**

Whether we fully understand it or not, the Power of Profit Motivation, as well as the powers of meditation and auto-suggestion, is a strong link with your future. You can use it to build your life and dreams.

Prepare Yourself for the Future

Are you ready?

If opportunity was offered to you tomorrow, would you recognize it? Would you know what to do with it? Could you estimate its worth?

Opportunity is constantly at the door, knocking for those who are listening at the *right* door. Find the right door for yourself and start listening. When opportunities first start coming to you, take each one, examine it closely and decide whether it fits your own needs. It might. It might not. But, you will learn two things by examining these opportunities as they come: You'll learn about what opportunities are available, and you'll learn more about your own needs and goals.

Thatcher K. found his door and started listening. Thatcher was the out-of-doors type and picked an appropriate door to stand near. He examined opportunities for herb farming, pheasant raising, trout farming, and apple growing before he decided on cooperative haying. And he started his business with zero dollars.

Thatcher knew many landowners in his rural area who had fields that went to hay each year but didn't have the equipment to harvest and bale it, and he heard opportunity knocking. Asking around, Thatcher found an equipment dealer in a nearby town who had horses and would gladly loan him a second-hand hay baler for a quarter of the hay he harvested with it. Thatcher then contacted farmers in his area who needed haying and charged them half of the hay he harvested for cutting and baling it. For an investment of his own time and gasoline Thatcher kept one quarter of all of the hay he cut. Thatcher soon had a ready market for the hay he kept, and he built his capital to the point where he bought the baler from the equipment dealer and was able to keep and sell half the hay he harvested.

Today, Thatcher runs a custom combine business in the Midwest where his huge harvest combines and crews move from farm to farm, harvesting crops for a percentage of the yield. Thatcher has also set up his own marketing system for the crops he retains and, as president of a four-state-wide corporation, earns nearly $75,000 a year. Thatcher started with no dollars—but a lot of sense.

Finding the right door to listen at is no more difficult than asking yourself what you would be most interested in doing. Are your interests in the rural life or the rush of city life? Do you enjoy sales work? Service work? Are you mechanically inclined? Do you work well with other people or do you prefer to work alone? What kind of opportunities appeal to you most?

When that opportunity does knock, be ready and able to recognize it for its worth and use it for your own profit.

BUILD YOUR FUTURE WITH
THE POWER OF PM

The Power of Profit Motivation is the power of the conscious and subconscious minds to clarify and act on well-defined problems and goals because they have been motivated to do so with a positive end result.

You've seen the Power of Profit Motivation work money miracles in the lives of others. You've seen the principles of Profit Motivation, meditation and auto-suggestion outlined before your mind. You've been shown the easy steps to a better tomorrow through the exploitation of the Power of Profit Motivation.

Take the challenge. Use the Power of PM in your own life. Grab hold of the future and make your dreams become realities with PM Power. *You* have the Power.

It's really up to *you*.

THINGS YOU CAN DO NOW

Procrastination has lost more fortunes than the stock market. Start today—right now—to plan your new life with the Power of Profit Motivation by doing these things:

1. **Decide what you want out of life. Write it down in words. Tell yourself what it would mean to you if your dreams were fulfilled tomorrow. How would it change your life? Be specific.**

2. **What financial goal will you set for yourself—$50,000 a year? More? Under what conditions would you like to earn it—At home? In a resort community? Traveling? How soon would you like to reach your goal? What short range goals can you set for yourself?**

3. Decide what type of opportunities for wealth appeal to you most. Is there one kind of opportunity that you would enjoy the most? What kind of profitable variations are there?

4. List your current assets· your talents, time and money. Decide how each of them can be used to help you reach your goal. How much of each of your assets are you willing to spend on your goal?

5. See yourself succeed. Envision yourself enjoying your wealth and happiness. Imagine yourself enjoying the luxuries you plan to have when you succeed: a new home, luxury cars, travel and more. Motivate yourself.

6. Meditate on the solution. Give your subconscious mind time to think. Take a moment once in awhile to relax and let your mind take you where it wishes within the framework of your desires. Tell yourself, "I have the Power within me to earn riches and find happiness greater than my dreams."

7. Think Profit Motivation.

2

Building

Your Fortune

with "GOLD"

GOLD can make you rich beyond your dreams.

I'm not referring to the metallic gold that is bought and sold in the world's exchanges. I'm talking about the **GOLD** that is even *more valuable*—the **GOLD** within you right now.

Here's my formula for **GOLD:**

G — Set your **GOALS.**
O — **ORGANIZE** your search.
L — **LOCATE** the right opportunity.
D — **DEVELOP** your opportunities into riches.

The Power of **GOLD**, like the Power of Profit Motivation, works within you every day to bring about positive change in your life. The Power of **GOLD** works more on the conscious level and gives you things you can do today—right now—to bring yourself closer to the riches you are searching for.

This chapter will show you how to put the Power of **GOLD** into your own life—you'll also learn how to use the other kind of gold to finance your money-making ventures with other people's resources.

GOLD—THE BASIS OF ALL WEALTH

Millions of people take life from beginning to end without going anywhere. They never know where they will be next year or even next month. They let life and other people buffet them around like a small sailboat in an ocean storm, never knowing if they will ever reach port. They have no compass, no sextant—no real goals.

Others—the successful—can tell you where they will be one year from now or even five years from now. They have a goal, a shining star, that they move towards, and by following that shiny star of tomorrow, they are bringing more light to today.

Which group would you rather be in? The *drifters* of life, who may or may not ever come closer to a better life, or the *doers*, who not only have the goal of a better life but are moving toward that goal and a better tomorrow?

GOLD can make the difference.

HOW THE POWER OF GOLD CAN MAKE YOU RICH

Whether your goal in life is an abundance of financial wealth, fame and notoriety, or freedom and independence, the Power of **GOLD** will help you reach your goal.

Roger T., at 27, had never heard of the **GOLD** Formula, but he knew the value of setting goals for himself. And he knew that he wanted to travel the world *before* he retired, not after. So, Roger set a goal of spending his 30's as a world traveler.

The first problem Roger had to face was how to raise enough cash to finance 10 years of traveling. The second was to decide how he was going to make a living for the rest of his life after he returned from his travels—and Roger had less than three years in which to find the answer.

He found it in two months.

Roger started looking the next day for ways of earning a living while he traveled. He decided on the merchant marines—at least for the first four years. Then, Roger planned to use savings from his sea-going job to finance the next two years of independent travels to ports he had missed during the previous four. The next two years—years seven and eight—he planned to travel as a crewman on yachts that sailed out of an Atlantic coast yachting club he had often visited as a young boy. For the final two years of his third decade, Roger expected to spend his time in a sea-going navigation school he had often read about in boating magazines, training for the day when he wanted a well-paying profession *with* the benefits of travel.

After setting and developing his goal, Roger found that he didn't need large savings to begin his ten-year adventure, so he decided to start it at 28 rather than wait until he was 30. Six years later, Roger is completing his independent travels and is looking forward to two years of travel on some wealthy person's yacht before he settles down to his schooling and life on the open sea.

Set your goal, organize your search, locate the right opportunity, then develop your opportunities into riches: those are the steps to GOLD.

Later in this book, I'll devote at least one chapter to each of the four steps in the **GOLD** Formula and show you the thousands of ways you can find riches with it. For now, I want you to see the Power of **GOLD** and what it can do *today* to change your entire life.

How to Set Your Goals for a Lifetime

Everyone has something in their life that they've always wanted to do, and most of these things take money. Whether you want to be a world traveler, as Roger did, or start your own trucking business, or live in a luxurious home in Beverly Hills, or set up a charitable organization for foster children, you're going to need money to get there. Not dirty, dishonest, stolen money, but fully earned and honestly gained riches that you can accumulate and spend with pride.

So, no matter what other goals you set for yourself in life, one of them should be the acquisition of a specific amount of money. It may be an income of $50,000 or more a year, or it may be a certain bank balance or financial worth, such as $1 million. Make this goal part of your life's goal, and your other goals will be fulfilled through motivation.

How Linda M. Changed Her Goals and Her Life

Linda M. had wanted to be a beautician for as long as she could remember. Linda graduated from high school in 1963 and could hardly wait to enroll in beauty school. She soon graduated and was working at her first shop. But, during the next 12 years, she worked at five different beauty shops, each no better or worse than the others. Linda decided she just wasn't getting anywhere and that maybe she should leave the beautician's trade and find something else—something with a little more challenge.

Fortunately, just before Linda took a job as a receptionist in a dentist's office, a friend asked Linda a question that would plague her for nearly two weeks:

"Why don't you open your own beauty shop, Linda? Janet did a couple years ago and now she has three of them and devotes most of her time to her ceramics hobby."

Well? Why not?

Linda had Profit Motivation. She found a goal.

Checking around, Linda found that one of her previous employers, Nadine W., was retiring as a beautician and was willing to sell her beauty shop on a contract. Linda withdrew most of her savings, took a personal loan for the balance of $1,500 and bought the Glamor Beauty Salon.

Today, Linda still works as head operator in her own four-chair salon and has plans to open another salon in a nearby suburban shopping center within two years. Linda still has a goal to work for, and it helps her enjoy *today* that much more.

Goals Can Be Changed

Even as a young boy, Bobby A. wanted to be a disc jockey. Bobby built a sound system from an old record player and speakers and entertained the neighborhood kids by mimicking the local radio stars. After graduation, Bobby enrolled in a broadcasting school and soon found himself in a small New Mexico town, working eight to 12 hours a day, six days a week, playing records, writing news stories and working on some of the broadcast equipment.

Two years later, Bobby was still working at the same station, doing the same thing for just about the same pay. Bobby found out that, while playing deejay was loads of fun, reaching the top—in both popularity and pay—would mean five to ten years of similar jobs before the "big break" *might* happen. He looked at his goal of being a big-time disc jockey again. Bobby decided that, at least for him, it wasn't worth the long years and low pay. But Bobby still enjoyed the entertainment field and decided to modify his goal.

Today, Bobby operates a talent agency in Los Angeles. He works not only with broadcast personalities, but also with major music stars. With nothing more than his first two months' office rent, Bobby started by placing a few of his more experienced broadcasting acquaintances into larger stations for a percentage of their income. Now, his income is nearly *six times* what it was as a deejay.

Setting the right goal is important, but often, even having a goal that you know you are going to have to modify someday will bring you closer to success than standing still.

How to Organize Your Search with GOLD

First, you set a goal—a shining star—that you are motivated towards. You can see it in your mind. You can see yourself enjoying what your goal will offer you. You know what you want, but you're not exactly sure how to get it.

That's when it's time to organize your search for the right path to your goal—a path that will bring you some of the rewards you are looking for, to be enjoyed today. It's time to plan each stepping stone along your path to wealth.

No matter what your financial goal is—$50,000 a year, $1,000,000 in the bank in ten years or a specific investment income for your retirement years—you can reach it by planning your work and working your plan.

Mike E. set his financial goal at earning exactly $1,000 a week, or $52,000 a year. He knew that the next step was to search for a way to bring his goal within reach. His arithmetic told him he had to earn $25 an hour for a 40 hour week to reach his goal. So he looked around him for opportunities that would offer him $25 an hour or more.

Mike found that many repairmen earned that much and more with just a basic mechanical aptitude and a few tools. He listed some of them: refrigeration repair, small-engine repair, automotive tune-up, amusement and vending-machine repair, cash register repair, lock and key service, saw-sharpening service and lawn mower rebuilding and resale.

By organizing his search for an opportunity that would fit his goals and desires, Mike found a well-paying business in which he could not only earn a top living without leaving his home shop, but also one he could enjoy: buying, repairing and reselling lawn mowers and other lawn equipment.

Mike continued his profitable search. He made a checklist of steps he would have to take to reach his financial goal:

_____ Check phone book and classified ads for competition.

_____ Talk with new lawn mower dealers for referrals.

_____ List necessary tools.

_____ Order business cards.

_____ Post business cards in shopping centers.

_____ Buy and repair a few old mowers.

_____ Resell mowers through classified ads.

_____ Estimate profit on first job.

_____ Buy next mowers estimating purchase price and resale value based on repairs at $25 an hour.

_____ Set up assembly and repair line in shop to speed rebuild.

_____ Develop referral and word-of-mouth business.

_____ Increase income and hire help.

Mike had the right idea: Organize your search for profits. He set his financial goal, then began searching for the best way to reach his goal, step-by-step.

Opportunity Knocks Often for Listeners

The man who first said, "Opportunity only knocks once," wasn't really listening. The people who make a handsome living from opportunities know that opportunity is knocking at your door nearly every day and that, rather than accept only the loudest opportunities, you can choose from the best of hundreds of opportunities to reach your profitable goal.

Locating opportunities is the key.

Your success in life is in direct relation to the number of opportunities you recognize and use to your own benefit

Today, you have the opportunity to talk with a banker about the best ways to finance your venture. Today, you can take an hour from your evening to develop the idea kicking around in your head about starting a particular business. Today, you can look into how a related business is being operated and at how profitably it is run. Today opportunity is knocking. Can you hear it?

John P. Was Listening

"I sure wish these salesmen would quit interrupting our day," Mr. Benjamin told his buyer, John P. "If we could just see them all at once, it would save both their time and mine."

Knock, knock.

John had an idea. Two weeks later, John had contacted similar buyers and the salesmen that regularly visited them and set up a weekly "Market Place." The "Market Place" was a small building near the industrial center where the manufacturers had their factories. It offered a weekly meeting place for buyers and sellers.

The "MarketPlace" flourished. Buyers spent one full day a week with salesmen and freed the other four days for other duties. Salesmen wasted less time on traveling between buyers and waiting to be seen. John earned a small percentage of everything sold within the "MarketPlace," cheerfully paid by the salesmen.

Soon John P. had different types of businesses booked every day of the week and offered the building to the public as a flea market on weekends. The "MarketPlace" offers John P. a salary of $70,000 a year—all because he heard opportunity knocking.

Start listening right now and—with the help of the Power of Profit Motivation—you'll begin hearing opportunity *hammering* at your door.

How to Build an Idea into a Fortune

An idea is worth *nothing*—until it is developed into something of value to someone else.

There are thousands of good ideas in the heads of people today that could make them wealthy beyond their imagination *if* they would only *develop* those ideas into the highly profitable ventures they could be. Maybe you have an idea right now that could easily bring "the good life" to you within weeks or months. All you might need is the knowledge of how to develop your idea into a *profitable* idea.

There are three steps to developing your idea into a fortune:

1. Make a list of all of the possible ways this idea could be used for profit.

2. Begin ruling out methods that are too costly in time or money, or may not bring a high-enough profit.

3. Put the odds in your favor by building the best method of your developed ideas into the fortune you want.

Bill C. was an unemployed bookkeeper. He was having trouble finding full-time work in his city, although many employers wanted a bookkeeper for a couple hours a week. So, Bill logically came up with the idea of renting his services out to many employers. He set up a schedule of businesses he visited with "Rent-A-Bookkeeper."

What a great idea, Bill thought. Why not develop it further for an even better profit.

Bill made a list: Rent-A-Gardener, -Housekeeper, -Companion, -Secretary, -Bartender, -Mechanic, -Clerk, -Attendant and so on. Bill asked around and found that some types of services were well covered and wouldn't be as profitable, but he came up with over a dozen Rent-A-Hand services that could be offered to businessmen, shut-ins and housewives. Bill began promoting his new business and is now looking to franchise his Rent-A-Hand business to other cities.

Bill had an idea that he felt would work, he made a list of profitable applications of the idea, ruled out the least likely and developed the rest into a highly profitable business that gives him a solid income plus the leisure time to enjoy it.

Bill C. knows how to develop a good idea into cash.

FINANCING YOUR FUTURE WITH GOLD

Credit—your ability to borrow money and pay it back—may be the biggest thing going for you on your way to riches. In fact, nearly every fortune ever made has been built with other people's money.

The principle of OPM (Other People's Money) goes like this: If you have found an opportunity to make 50 percent on an investment of your own money, why not borrow 10 times more at 10 or 15 percent and multiply your profit to between 400 and 450 percent of your original investment? Keep the difference for your ingenuity.

Doris T. found a bargain: 200 handbags imported from Italy that were being sold at a public auction she attended with a friend. When she saw that they were going to be sold for $380, she decided to take a chance on a big profit. Doris successfully bid $400 for the lot. She only had $100 with her as a deposit, so she started looking for the remaining $300 with the motivation that she could easily triple her money in a few months.

Doris used her bank card to get a fast $200 loan at three percent a month, then borrowed $100 from a friend, promising to pay $125 in three months. The 200 imported bags were soon in her dining room.

Doris began selling the bags, which she found were offered in finer shops for $30 each, to friends, co-workers and neighbors at $12 each. They went faster than Doris had expected and three weeks after the public sale Doris had sold all 200 purses for a clear profit of $1,969. That is a profit of almost *2,000 percent* on her original investment in less than a month because Doris knew how to use her credit to increase her profit leverage.

HOW TO MAKE YOUR CREDIT WORK FOR YOU

There are many honest things you can do to help your credit rating and thereby help your chances for success with your own profitable venture.

Income: Document your income with a letter from your employer or other source. They will often include money earned in overtime and irregular sources that the finance company might not have added in to compute your total income. Also, be sure to ask for a reference letter from your employer if possible, showing you as a conscientious worker with a good record. This will often help you with your loan application.

Stability: List your employment, leaving out any jobs that were of a short duration. You will want to show an increase in responsibilities and income from each succeeding job to earn the best credit. If you have changed fields in the last two years, show how your former and current occupation are related if possible.

Obligations: Remember, you don't need to list any obligations on your credit application that you expect to pay off with the proceeds of your loan. You *can* list them under credit references. In fact, you may want to consolidate or refinance a few of your bills as you apply for your new loan.

By doing so, you will be decreasing your obligations while keeping your credit at the higher level, thus allowing for a better loan.

Use for money: You don't have to tell your lending institution exactly what you are planning to use your loan proceeds for. You can specify "major purchase," "debt consolidation," "vacation fund," "investment," or one of a number of other things. As long as you are promising to pay back the money you borrow—with interest—it's really up to you how you spend it. If you feel you have a venture that you think the lender would be interested in hearing about, be sure to document every expectation you have for profits before you apply in order to insure the best impression.

Where to Find Capital for Your Ventures

There are hundreds of places you can find the capital you may need to get your profitable venture off the ground. Some of them, like savings, banks and small business loan associations, are quite obvious. But there are dozens more you might have overlooked. Don't pass up any possibility for financing your high-profit idea.

Investment fund: Florence C. began her first venture, Cookie Jar Investment Company, with a cookie jar. For six months, while an idea brewed in her mind for a profitable home business, Florence would put change and bills into a cookie jar as she could afford it. After six months, her idea was ready and her funds totaled $342.10.

Today Florence C. earns over $25,000 a year with her spare-time business by making plaques for the kitchen. Her initial investment saved in a cookie jar, gave her both a financial start and the name of her firm.

Saving accounts: Many small investors will first look to their savings, realizing that it is much better to earn 25%, 100%, 1000% or more on their money than the 6% or more that savings and loans offer. How much you can take from savings for your venture depends on two things: how much you can afford to risk and how much you want to earn.

Loans against savings: Most savings and loan associations will also offer you the best of both worlds by issuing a loan that uses your savings accounts as collateral. They usually charge about two percent above what your account is earning, but for many investors, this kind of loan offers both security and liquid funds.

A variation of this financial source is using someone else's savings account as collateral for a loan. Friends, relatives and even strangers are often willing to use their savings account to back up your loan for a small fee.

Get off Your Assets

Home equity loans and second mortgages: If you are making payments on your own home you may have accumulated enough equity or appreciation in your property to apply for a home equity loan. A home equity loan often offers about 70% of the difference between your current mortgage balance and your home's market value. For many who have lived in their own homes for three years or more, or live in an area where home values are increasing quickly this could mean thousands of dollars that can be used for your profitable ideas.

Or, you can take a second mortgage out against your real estate to finance a business venture. Many small businesses have been started with this type of capital. Ask your banker.

Car and boat loans: The idea of borrowing against what you already own—your assets—can be carried farther to include other major property such as your car, boat, motor home or travel trailer. Many banks and finance companies can quote you the cost of such a loan. Shop for the lowest financing rates as you would shop for the lowest food prices.

Banks, savings & loans and other loan firms: Your signature is often good enough collateral for a loan of a few hundred to a few thousand dollars. In general, finance companies are the easiest to secure loans with, but often require higher interest rates. Commercial banks are next, especially if you have had an established checking or savings account with them for awhile. They are usually looking for short-term loans (four years and under). Savings and loan associations prefer longer term loans such as mortgages, but their rates are lower if you qualify. Also, look to credit unions. Some credit unions are very easy to get along with, offering the capital availability of a finance company with the amiability of a bank.

SBA loans: The federal government's Small Business Administration has millions of dollars in capital to offer to businesses that have difficulty finding capital with other sources. The SBA also has booklets on how to run small businesses profitably. A call or visit to your SBA office, located in many metropolitan cities, may be worth thousands of dollars to you.

Mail-order loans: The higher the interest you are willing to pay, the easier it is to find a lender. Dozens of reputable mail-order loan companies advertise each month in the mechanics magazines and tabloid newspapers. If your credit is fair and you need less than $5,000, write to one of these mail-order loan companies to see if you qualify for financing.

Bank cards: You may have a few hundred dollars of quick, ready cash in your wallet right now, in the form of bank cards. Most bank cards offer you "instant cash" of up to $500 by presenting your card at a participating bank. Don't overlook this source for small but easy capital for a venture that can turn other people's money into high profits for you. In addition, some banks offer coverage of an overdrawn check to a specified limit. If you have such an account, list it among your sources for capital.

Advertise for loans: Most daily newspapers carry a classified section column under "Investment Capital Wanted" or a similar heading. Under it, you will find people who are willing to pay 10, 15 and even 25 percent and more in interest to secure loans for what they feel are profitable business ventures. Read the ads. Decide which ads are most successful in gaining the attention of investors, then write a similar ad for your venture. Don't overlook the other "Investment Capital" column, the one offering money to entrepreneurs.

Private stock investment groups: After checking with your state's securities commission, you may consider selling stock in your business venture if your capital needs are over $5,000. The concept is simple: decide on how much capital you will need, divide that number by the number of investors you feel would be interested in buying stock (friends, relatives, professional people, other investors), issue that number of stocks, write a prospectus or report on your venture and start selling the stock.

Michael V. wanted to start a recording company. He needed $35,000 to set up and operate his business for six months. Michael felt he could interest 30 to 40 friends and people in the recording business into buying stock so he issued 3500 shares at $10 each. Four years later the shares were worth $28.50 each. Investors nearly tripled their money in four years and are anxious to buy into Michael's next stock sale.

Friends and relatives: Thousands of enterprising people have begun their fortunes with money borrowed from friends and relatives. In many cases, they are the easiest financiers to please and are more-than-willing to offer a helping hand to someone starting out in business. Check with them first. Chances are that one or more of your "rich uncles" started his fortune with capital borrowed from relatives. Don't pass this method by.

Get a raise: Another method of obtaining venture capital is by earning a raise in pay at your current job. With a little application and additional conscientious work, most employees can soon earn raises. If your regular job is built on an inflexible scale of pay, think about how you can earn honest overtime by working evenings, weekends and holidays. Then be sure to use these extra dollars solely for your new business venture rather than luxuries.

Get a second job: You can gather $2,000 to $10,000 in capital that you won't have to pay back with a part-time job. It may be in a field related to your everyday work, or it may be in a completely unrelated field. In any case, check the help wanted column every day and you'll soon find a part-time job that will bring you the extra cash you need to get ahead— and stay ahead—of your co-workers who have less ingenuity and drive.

Get a partner: You have the intelligence and determination to find a worthwhile fortune. There are others who have a start on their fortune but lack the business ability and ideas you can offer. Make a team that will take you both where you want to go. Start looking for a partner who offers both the cash reserves and the complementary skills you will need to make your venture profitable. You can look through classified sections, ask among friends and co-workers, talk to bankers and professional people and listen to others. Keep in mind that a partnership is much like a marriage—its outcome depends on your choice of a partner.

Sell something of value: I've talked about both earning and borrowing money. Something should be said about raising capital for your venture through selling valuables. Most of us collect things that we've always wanted but soon tire of. There is often good profit-making capital tied up in things of value that we no longer use. Check your garage and attic for things that can be sold for cash to help start your new venture. You may find garage sale items, appliances that are still in good working condition, antiques, long-forgotten toys, sporting goods, automotive parts, furniture and more that can turn into quick cash. Your neglected valuables may bring you a few hundred or a few thousand dollars—possibly enough cash to start a high-profit business that will someday offer you even more valuables.

GOLD is everywhere.

Set your goals, organize your search, locate the right opportunity, then develop it into wealth by using the power of other people's riches to make riches of your own. It's all waiting for you when you use the Power of Profit Motivation and my formula for **GOLD**.

THINGS YOU CAN DO NOW

You are *wealth*. You have the intelligence, creativity, drive and power it takes to earn wealth that only a few ever enjoy. Unlock your life and your mind to the **GOLD** within you *right now* by doing these things:

1. **Study the GOLD Success Formula.** Within its four points are the steps to your future. Show yourself why these four steps can lead you to riches. See yourself enjoying the financial wealth you've always dreamed of.

2. **Think about your specific goals in life.** How much money will make you happy?—$50,000 a year? $100,000? A net worth of $1,000,000? Ask yourself just how much you want out of life. Give serious thought to the goals you want to set for yourself.

3. **Begin organizing your time and your thoughts.** If you have something you've always wanted to do—write a story, study a subject, build a sailboat or lose a few pounds—start planning right now how you are going to do it. Then work your plan. Prove to yourself how organization and determination can get things done in your life.

4. Start looking for opportunities. Begin reading the financial columns in your daily newspaper. Check the classified ads for investors and investments. Talk to friends about business and success. Write for information on business ventures offered in ads.

5. Look for financing. Build your credit rating and have ideas in reserve on how you could raise $100, $500, $1,000, $5,000 or more in a short time if you needed it for a profitable business venture.

6. Put it all together and *be ready* to take calculated risks when you see a method of making high profits. Be ready to move when things happen.

7. Think Profit Motivation.

3

How to Set
Your
Profit Targets

This is the most important chapter in this book. In it, you are going to learn two very important things:

1. How to set your life's financial goals, and
2. How to develop the skills you need to reach them.

Let's get down to business.

FIND YOUR MONEY GOALS

The first two chapters of this book have prodded you to consider how much money it will take to bring you happiness, but you probably haven't set your specific goal yet.

You will now, with the help of your own *Wealth Worksheet*. You are going to analyze your own needs for both today and tomorrow. You are going to look at your own investment and the rewards you can expect. You are going to find ways of reaching your financial goals within a specific amount of time.

This chapter can easily be worth thousands of dollars to you.

Life hadn't been too easy for Fletcher R. He started out at the wrong end of town, where ambition was laughed at. Fletcher found a job setting pins in a bowling alley after school to earn money for the family.

Fletcher R. was 26 before he set his first goal. After a dozen years on the job market, Fletcher saw that a man with no particular skills was destined to repeat his parents' life. With a wife and two children to support, Fletcher decided he needed a skill.

Fletcher was 30 before he finally did something about it and took a job as an apprentice welder in a factory where he had formerly been a shipping clerk. His salary nearly doubled, but Fletcher wanted more.

One day in 1964, Fletcher R. sat down to talk it over with himself. What did he want? What could he do? Where did he want to go? Fletcher wrote his goal down on paper: He wanted to own his own welding shop and earn at least $15,000 a year by 1969. How was he going to reach that goal? He figured he could do it by working a second job in a welding shop and saving his second income to start his own shop. This time, Fletcher didn't put it off for four years— he started toward his new goal the next day.

In July of 1968, Fletcher's opportunity came. The owner of the shop where he worked evenings decided to retire. He offered to sell Fletcher his entire welding shop with an established clientele—all of whom Fletcher knew personally—for $10,000 down and payment of $250 a month. If Fletcher R. had not sat down and developed his financial goal and road to success back in 1964 he would not have been ready. But Fletcher *was* ready. He bought out his old boss, and within two months of the goal date he had set five years earlier, Fletcher was earning $15,000 a year. Since then, Fletcher has set more goals for himself and his new business. Fletcher feels that the most important thing he ever learned was how to set goals. He will gladly tell you that, thanks to goal-setting, his children will never see the other side of the tracks as he saw them.

You'll be setting your own goals within your Wealth Worksheet soon, but first you'll need to know more about financial goals.

Four Ways to Wealth

There are four types of financial goals you can set for yourself.

Income goals: You may look at your financial needs and decide that a certain income, say $50,000 a year or more, will satisfy your needs. You are then setting an Income Goal. You have decided that $1,000 a week in income would offer you the things from life that you've always wanted and felt you deserved. Or, your goal may be $75,000 a year or more. Whatever it is, you are setting a specific goal of short-term wealth accumulation and can expect the best from life when you reach it.

Equity goals: Your goal may be the accumulation of a certain amount of wealth: $250,000, $500,000, $1,000,000 or even more. You are willing to work and strive for your long-term goal, expecting to be able to relax at the end and never have to worry about money problems again. Equity goals take more stamina, but can be more rewarding in later years. As others continue to work for their income goals each year, your equity goal has been reached, and you are enjoying its many benefits.

Income-to-equity goals: This type of money goal uses "surplus money" or income to invest in equity-building wealth. An example is someone who takes all income over $1200 a month and invests it in moderate risk real estate and stock ventures. That person is building equity or worth much faster than he or she would by putting that surplus money in a bank or savings and loan account. Many millionaires who started small built their fortunes this way.

Equity-to-income goals: This kind of goal gives you the opportunity to build a large amount of equity or net worth—such as $1,000,000—which is then re-invested to give you a regular income. This is often done with people who earn a large sum in a short time. They use most of their new fortune as an investment in real estate or the stock market which can offer them a regular income for many years.

Each of these four types of financial goals has its own advantages and disadvantages. Much depends on what you need and desire from life. Security? Prosperity? A steady income? A retirement fund? A major purchase such as a home, car or college education in a certain number of years? Take a close look at your financial needs and your goals will be easier to set.

How to Analyze Your Financial Needs

It's time to start building your future with your own *Wealth Worksheet.* Your Wealth Worksheet will help you visualize your financial needs today and tomorrow as well as help you set goals that will bring you freedom and security as you have never known. Take out a blank piece of paper, label it "Wealth Worksheet" and answer the questions on the next few pages.

What are your financial needs *today*? Food, shelter, clothing and transportation. What else? Past obligations and bills, special charities, hobbies? Estimate the amount of dollars it takes for you to live as you live today.

How about *tomorrow*? Would you like to move into a larger home in the next five years? What kind of down payment will you need? Monthly payments? How much will your luxuries cost? How many inflated dollars will it take to give you the things you want to have five years from now?

SET YOUR GOALS WITH YOUR WEALTH WORKSHEET

You've outlined today's needs and tomorrow's desires on your Wealth Worksheet. How are you going to earn that money? With income goals? Income-to-equity goals? A business of your own? Raises at your present job? An additional job?

As you set your goals remember to:

- Be specific.
- Be realistic.
- Make them attainable.
- Make them desirable.
- Make them believable.
- Make them measurable.
- Make them challenging.
- List them by priority.
- Set specific completion dates.

Remember that a life of success is the sum total of daily successes.

HOW TO INVEST IN TOMORROW

How many hours do you have available each day, week or month that can be invested in your financial future? Two? Five? Eight? Twenty? More? In lieu of money, time is the best investment you can make toward your financial goals. Each hour you spend now in building your fortune is worth more than the money you could probably invest in your

enterprise. Each hour you give to your financial future now
may be worth $15, $25, $50 or even $100 in additional income later. Invest what you have the most of: time. Look to
the start of the day. Can you rise an hour earlier to plan and
work on your fortune? Can you borrow two hours each
evening or a few hours over the weekend to start your
enterprise of wealth? These precious hours are as good as
gold when you invest them in your future.

Second to time, you'll want to invest capital into your
new enterprise. How much can you afford to invest? $10 a
month? $25? $100? More? Begin saving for your investment
right now, and when you find the *right* enterprise you'll have
the resources to capitalize on the opportunity.

Plan to invest both your spare time and money in your
future and you'll soon be among the thousands of people
who earn vast fortunes through the Power of Profit
Motivation and their own ingenuity.

WRITE YOUR OWN FINANCIAL TICKET

Your Wealth Worksheet shows you many things: what
you need today, what you want from tomorrow and what
you can invest in your future. It even offers methods of
reaching your goal. You Wealth Worksheet may be the most
important form you'll ever fill out.

Do it now. Put it all down in black and white. Write out
your own goals as you see them today. Fill out your personal
Wealth Worksheet, fold it and put it in your pocket or purse
to be kept with you at all times. Take it out every day. Look
at it. Make positive revisions if necessary. Don't let it go.

When you have a quiet moment to spare, take out your
Wealth Worksheet and allow the Power of Profit
Motivation to help you make your dreams and goals come
true. Concentrate on your financial goals and see yourself
enjoying their benefits: a finer home, a newer car, prestige,

travel or whatever you want your fortune to offer you. Then, think about the steps you'll need to take to get there. Will you invest time? Money? How much? Make short-range goals and deadlines that will bring you closer to your long-range goal. Set specific completion dates and plan to meet them.

BUILD YOUR PROFITABLE SKILLS

Every living person has or can acquire at least one skill that can be turned into a high-profit venture. That's right. You have skills or potential skills that you are using right now that can bring you the wealth and prosperity you just outlined in your Wealth Worksheet.

Take a second sheet of paper, label it "Skills Worksheet" and answer questions raised on the next few pages.

How to Profit from Things You Do

Let's list some of the special skills that you have. Think about your regular job for a moment, whether you're a bricklayer, a housewife or even if you're currently un-employed. There are certain skills that you have acquired over the years that many people would like to have. What are they? List your physical skills such as carpentry, auto repair, cooking, electronics, truck driving, cement work and so on. Then, think about your mental skills: bookkeeping, organization, research, salesmanship and others. Do you have the special skill of getting along well with others? Write that down, too, on your Skills Worksheet.

Look at both the jobs you have now and the jobs you've had in the past.

Frank M. is a body and fender man. He has worked in the same shop for ten years and is highly skilled. Before that, Frank drove a truck for a national trucking company. These are two of the skills that Frank wrote down on his Skills Worksheet: auto body repair and truck driving. His way to wealth could be through a combination of these two skills such as a truck body repair or a portable auto body shop. Or, Frank could decide to leave his current trade and return to truck driving for more income. The more skills you have, the more wealth combinations you can come up with. List your current work skills on your Skills Worksheet right now.

How to Profit from Things Your Enjoy

Do you collect coins, stamps, antiques, butterflies, radiator caps, old photos, stained glass, bottles or anything else? If so, you probably have another marketable skill. Be sure to include this skill or special knowledge on your Skills Worksheet.

In Chapter 4, I'll tell you about Art D., whose interest in coin collecting during high school led him to his own highly profitable business.

Are there past hobbies that you can list among your skills? Maybe you once built a large and impressive collection of beer cans or photos of early California. You can still turn these hobbies into cash with just a short refresher course. Think about it. Do you have any hobby skills that have been neglected? Write them down.

How about other interests? Have you always held a secret desire to get into broadcasting, or operate a bus service, or learn to be a master chef, or have your own professional fishing boat on the Pacific? Do you have a pleasant voice, a bus driver's license, cooking ability or a knowledge of coastal fishing that could be turned into profit? Don't forget to list your skills of interest on your Skills Worksheet.

Improve Your Skills for Profit

You've probably come up with a list of skills that run in every direction of human endeavor. Some are highly specialized and some are general skills that could be taken to nearly any profession you enter. Some of these skills will need no development to be profitable, while others will need some refinement to bring you the riches you are looking for.

Which of these skills can be improved with further education? Mark them with an "X" on your Skills Worksheet. Which ones are you most interested in developing through education? Circle those "X"s with an "O." Then let's look at the ways these skills can be developed to your profit.

Schools: If you have finished high school, the next logical step for these skills is college if courses are available. You need not try for a degree, but can take only the courses you need to improve your particular skills. If you haven't finished high school, speak with a local school counselor about developing your skills with future education.

Night courses: Millions of adults are back in school attending night classes in everything from welding to creative stitchery to accounting principles. In fact, this is where most adults pick up new skills and dust off the old ones they have.

Tony L. put "art" down on his Skills Worksheet. He had always been interested in art and felt he had some talent, but had no formal training. Tony saw art as a possible road to wealth and happiness, so he started his future with art courses at a local adult education program. Tony started his investment fund with money earned from calligraphy and signs. Within a year Tony felt he was ready and opened his own studio gallery in a turn-of-the-century house near the business district of his town. Today, Tony still owns and operates the Creative Brush Gallery where his and other paintings sell for $250 to $1,000 each—all because Tony decided to go back to school.

Correspondence courses: Sometimes it's just too difficult to attend school because of time or distance. Many people try correspondence courses to improve their skills. There are courses available in veterinary clinic work, automotive customizing and painting, becoming a travel agent, millwright skills, tax accounting and a thousand other easily learned skills.

Correspondence courses are for those who don't have trouble studying. Instructors can usually help you motivate yourself and set up your study schedule to get the most out of the course. Most magazines will have ads for dozens of correspondence schools. One of them might offer you the skill you need to reach your goals.

Self-study: Often, the hardest method, self-study, is also the least expensive and most flexible. Setting up your own study plan will let you tailor your educational needs to your time and methods. It does require that you are a self-motivator who can shut out distractions and learn without outside help.

With self-study, you can also try to get someone who is accomplished in the field you are studying to show you the best books and methods to learn your skill. In fact, they may have some of the books you will need to study. Self-education allows you to set up your study schedule around any other activities or jobs you might have.

How to Find Your Most Profitable Skills

Some skills will bring you riches faster than others. Business administration and sales skills will often bring wealth much quicker than manual skills such as plumbing, auto repair and machine work. In other words, skills of the mind offer a greater potential for wealth than skills of the muscles. A combination of the two, however, can bring you wealth beyond the sum of the two.

Eileen U. is a seamstress, and a very good one. Eileen often put in 10, 12 and 14 hours a day trying to keep up with business. Soon, Eileen realized that she was moving fast, but getting nowhere. She had $2,000 in the bank but wanted to find a way to earn 10 times as much while still allowing time in her life to enjoy some of it. She looked hard at the problem.

Eileen talked with her husband, Gary. He suggested that she needed a course in business administration. Eileen waited until her slower season, then enrolled in a small business administration course at a nearby community college.

During the sixth week of classes, it hit her; Why not hire others as apprentice seamstresses, train them to her satisfaction and operate her business like a real business.

She did. Today, Eileen operates a seamstress shop in her converted garage and employs three women. None of the four works more than 40 hours a week, and they all earn a very good living—especially Eileen, the smart one.

Develop proficiencies of your mind. Learn as much as you can about management skills, accounting and income tax, salesmanship, administration, positive mental attitude and financial opportunities.

Your Skills Worksheet Offers the Key to Tomorrow

Use your Skills Worksheet to plan both your future and the steps you will take toward that future. Look over the skills you have listed and review them in your mind.

- How would you rate each one—Excellent? Good? Fair?
- Which ones need the least development? The most?
- Which skills do you feel most comfortable with?
- Which ones will bring you the success you are looking for?
- What combinations can you make with these skills?
- How can you improve your most profitable skills?
- Who can you talk to about your education?
- What kind of educational facilities are available to you?
- How have others used your skills to build their wealth?

Study your Skills Worksheet very carefully. It could be your golden key to a future of wealth, prosperity and happiness.

SKILLS YOU WILL NEED TO SUCCEED

There are hundreds of skills that you will need to take you to complete success, but most of them can be put into a few general categories for study. Those skills are:

- The ability to be a self-starter.
- The ability to organize your time and work.
- The ability to research and test your ideas.
- The ability to handle financial information.
- The ability to get along with other people.
- The ability to motivate others to help you.
- The ability to make decisions.

Be a Self-Motivator

To motivate others to give you money for something you do for them, you must first motivate yourself to work to earn that money. You must give a little push to yourself and say, "I won't find wealth unless I *earn* wealth." You must motivate yourself.

As Chapter 1 has shown, one of the best self-motivators in our society is Profit Motivation, working with an eye on the reward rather than the chore. If you've studied the lives of the great capitalists like Carnegie, Getty, Rockefeller, Melon, Hughes and others, you've seen the pattern. That pattern is self-motivation. These successful and wealthy people all had one thing in common: They knew how to find the goal posts, then pushed themselves towards them.

You can apply the same skill, the same ability. You can be a self-motivator.

Self-motivation is not a gift or a blessing. It is a learned skill that can be developed with ideas presented earlier in this book and the Power of Profit Motivation. How much would a $50,000 a year income at home really mean to you? What would it give you? Is the reward large enough to make you invest the comparatively small amount of time and money you will need to achieve it? If so, you have self-motivation. You have Profit Motivation.

How to Organize Your Plan

"Planning your work and working your plan" is more than just an old platitude, it's a skill you will need on your way to your fortune. You and your neighbor and your boss and a man in Perth, Australia, all have one thing in common: Your days all contain exactly 24 hours in them, no more and no less. What each of you do with those 24 hours is what separates the rich from the poor, the happy from the unhappy, and the doers from the done-to.

Once you have set your personal goal, that of earning a certain number of dollars in a certain amount of time, your organizational skills will decide whether you get there.

Frank A. set his goal at $50,000 a year from a home-operated business within two years. Great! But how was he going to get there? By using short divison, Frank found that $50,000 a year is $25 an hour for a 40 hour week, working 50 weeks a year. So, Frank's wealth plan went something like this:

- 1 month—Find part-time business that pays $25 an hour.
- 2 months—Begin operating business 12 hours a week.
- 6 months—Build business to 15 hours a week at $25 hr.
- 1 year— Build business to 20 hours a week at $25 hr.
- 1 ½ years—Leave regular job and work 30 hours a week at new business.
- 2 years—Build business to 40 hours a week at $25 hr.

Then Frank began filling in the blank spaces in his wealth plan. He started looking for a part-time business that could offer him $25 an hour. Frank found many more than he thought he would: auto repair, special equipment repair, product sales, business consultation service, light manufacturing and others. Frank finally decided on the business he felt would be the most profitable and that he would enjoy running.

Today, Frank is operating his business 30 hours a week from his garage, making concrete lawn statues and earning nearly $40,000 a year.

Once you have a goal, organize your search for the best method, then organize your method for the best profits. More on organization in the next chapter.

How to Test Your Ideas

Another skill you will want to acquire on your road to riches is research and marketing. Research and marketing is simply finding out, beforehand, whether anyone will actually use your product or service, who they are and how you can reach them. Thousands of businesses fail each year because of the lack of these two skills. You can have the greatest business idea in the world, but if no one wants it or you don't know how to reach those who do, your business has a poor chance of succeeding.

Research and marketing can also be defined as need and motivation. You first have to find out if there is a need for your business, and then you must motivate others to use it. Often overlooked by the new businessperson, research and marketing are skills that are highly developed in the successful business entrepreneur.

How to Handle High Finance

The largest single reason why businesses fail is lack of recordkeeping. Hundreds of thousands of small business people think that bookkeeping and accounting are only for income tax purposes, which is entirely wrong. Record-keeping is for the business *operator*, and it helps you not only to know how much you made or lost in operating your business, but it also shows you how and where you earned and lost it. "The books" are the pulse of every business. To keep an eye on the health of your business, it's a good idea to check your pulse—your books—regularly.

Decide to build your financial skills now. If you feel uncomfortable with math, spend a few hours each week for a month on brushing up your mathematics skills. Your local librarian has many books on elementary math for adults.

Take a course in business or bookkeeping if you can. If not, get a book on the subject to acquaint you with the terms you'll be coming across when you own your business: accrual, depreciation, economic life, p & l statement, debit and credit, amortization, discounted paper, capital assets and a hundred others. Everything you learn that will help you operate your business more efficiently will put more money in your pocket and pay you back many times over.

Learn to Like People

People are your profits. Whether you make your fortune with a wholesale or retail business, a service or a product, people—in every size, shape and style—will be your customers, and how well you work with these people will have much to do with your success.

One of the skills you will want to develop as you build your fortune is working for and with people. You'll want to know how to read their needs and offer them what they want. You'll want to keep them happy, so they will bring their business back to you. You'll want to learn how to get the most out of people, especially employees. You'll not only want to be an expert in your own business field, but you'll also want to be an expert on the people who use your business.

Learn to enjoy people—they are your profits.

How to Motivate People

As William Exton says in his book, *Motivational Leverage: A New Approach to Managing People* (Parker Publishing Co., Inc., West Nyack, New York), "The greatest advantage you can have in getting what you want out of life is the ability to influence others." In fact, how you influence others may determine success or failure in your own wealth enterprise. You must not only like people, but you must also know how to motivate them to do what you want them to do. Whether you are dealing with the supplier, customer, banker or employee, you will be able to profit from each more effectively as you develop the skill of motivating others.

Be a Decision-Maker

Some people always know the right thing to do at the right time—but success eludes them because they never decide to act. They don't know how to make decisions.

Decision-making is also an acquired skill. It can be developed in anyone who is willing to weigh facts and develop them objectively against their own needs.

Martin L. always wanted to invest in real estate. He felt that buying income property was the best method of building wealth for the future. He wasn't sure exactly what type of property he wanted to invest in, but he was sure he wanted something that would make him money.

One day, a real estate broker-friend brought him information on a property that had just come on the market. It was a commercial building in a busy location. It had three units, all leased for two to five years. The current owner was willing to sell the building on a contract with only 15 percent down and lease payments would more than pay the mortgage payments, giving Martin some income and offering him an equity-building business that needed little management.

Martin had enough for the down payment, but couldn't decide whether to purchase the property or buy a new car he wanted. "I'll give you my answer in a couple of weeks," he told the broker.

A week later, the property was sold to a more decisive person who knew not only the value of the property, but also knew that it fit his financial needs very well. He didn't wait for opportunity to knock a second time, and he doesn't regret his move because the building has appreciated over 20 percent a year for the last two years.

Martin made a big decision—the wrong one—when he tried to put the decision off. Decision-making is a necessary skill that can be developed for high profit and long-term wealth.

These are the skills you will need in almost any enterprise you decide on, and you can develop any or all of them by applying yourself to their basic principles and practicing them in your everyday life.

If profit is your target, financial goals and business skills are your ammunition.

THINGS YOU CAN DO NOW

Without goals, football would be a game of big men running around in circles. Without goals, life isn't much different. Set your financial goals and develop your skills *right now* by doing these things:

1. Decide on your own financial goals. The talking is over. It's time to make a firm decision on just how much wealth you want from life. Write down an exact figure.

2. Complete your Wealth Worksheet. Make sure you know your profit target and how you plan to aim at it. Use your Wealth Worksheet to outline your plan for bringing vast riches to your life.

3. Analyze your skills. Without the right kind of business skills, you may never reach the top of the financial mountain. Don't settle for the foothills—build your skills with Profit Motivation.

4. Complete your Skills Worksheet. Find out just what you can do and what you need to do to bring the wealth you are searching for. What are you going to do about the skills you need but lack?

5. Develop your needed skills. Educate yourself. Find out what skills you need for success and *go after them.* Every skill you develop may mean an extra $10,000, $50,000 or even $250,000 to you.

6. Think Profit Motivation.

4

The Tactics

of

Profit Search

Millions of dollars in easy profits are within your reach right now.

That's right. There are hundreds of purely honest and fantastically profitable ideas so close to you right now that you'd be ecstatic if you could see them all.

And you *can* see them if you look with the fresh concept of Profit Motivation in mind. Start looking right now and, if you know *how* to look, you'll find at least one highly profitable idea in the next five minutes that could catapult you to riches and success beyond your imagination.

How can you recognize these potential profits? By simply looking for them with a Profit-Motivated eye and

studying them thoroughly with a Profit-Motivated mind.
It's that easy.

SAM C. TURNS A LOSS INTO A PROFIT

Sam C. was a heavy equipment operator — until an accident made him look for other work. Sam didn't have a college education, or a second trade or any training that would give him and his family a living.

But, Sam had a feeling for Profit Motivation. He could see enterprise in things that no one else dreamed of. So, laid off from his last job with no prospects for another, Sam sat down to think it all out.

He took out a scratch pad.

"I'm looking for something that sells for at least four times its cost, can be made in my basement without any special skills and can be started with just a few dollars' investment."

Sam picked up the classified section from a local daily newspaper for ideas.

"That's it! I've got it!" Right in front of his eyes he saw thousands of people who were willing to shell out $5 or more for a classified ad in hopes of selling something they were either making or no longer had use for.

Sam started figuring. If he only got *ten percent* of the ads at *half the price* this classified section received, he could make a fantastic living without having to leave home.

Problem: Sam knew nothing about printing or publishing. But, his wife Joyce was a secretary and knew how to type and run a mimeograph machine. That afternoon, Sam went to the library and checked out every book he could find on printing, advertising, distribution methods and promotion.

A few weeks later, with just $300 of their own money, Sam and Joyce mimeographed their first small classified ad paper to serve their suburban community.

Eight years later, Sam's "small" publication was reaching over 100,000 homes every week and his business was valued at nearly $1 million. Sam not only owned the building his new office was in, but he also owned all of the buildings on his block as well as the one across the street which housed his new $150,000 press.

All this happened because Sam knew how to use Profit Motivation.

SEVEN WAYS TO WEALTH

You can come up with hundreds of profitable business ideas by just reviewing these seven ways to wealth:

1. Your regular job.
2. Related jobs.
3. Your hobbies or interests.
4. Your previous training or education.
5. Your friends and acquaintances.
6. Popular fads.
7. Brainstorming.

Today's Job is Tomorrow's Opportunity

The most obvious place to start looking for wealth is with your own full-time job. Whether you're an architect, a clerk-typist or a housewife, your greatest chance for riches is in the field you know the best. So, start looking at your own livelihood for the best and most profitable way of working toward your goal of earning over $50,000 a year at home.

Frank G. was a bricklayer who was about to retire on a pension that was barely adequate. Frank was no longer young, but with nearly 50 years' experience as a bricklayer Frank knew his job as no one else did. What Frank lacked in stamina he made up for in experience. So, he decided to start using his brains and someone else's brawn.

Frank teamed up with two young bricklayers who were willing to work for 80 percent of their regular fee if they could have enough jobs to keep them busy most of the year.

Frank drew on the hundreds of contacts he had met during his half-century in the construction business, and he soon had a waiting list of profitable jobs for the two young men. They gladly paid Frank 20 percent each for lining up the jobs.

In two years, Frank was subcontracting for six energetic bricklayers and was taking home more money than he ever had before. His job took only 1 ½ days a week and he found he could do most of his work over his home phone.

Frank would often scratch his head, wondering why he hadn't thought of his lucrative business sooner in life.

Mini-Businesses Yield Maxi-Profits

There are lots of other ways of turning your present job into a full-time, profit-making business.

Large corporations are often cold and businesslike. People still like the human touch and will often spend more with businessmen who will make them feel that their business is appreciated. You may see this often at your present job. You may be able to start your own profitable business at home using "personalized service" as your motto. You renew the human side to enterprise for your customers by being president, secretary *and* complaint department in your own business — a scaled-down version of a larger firm.

Or, you may decide to stay on the friendliest of terms with your ex-bosses when you leave your current job with the idea of sub-contracting work from them.

Marvin L. owns his own trucking company — a $2 million-a-year business, operated out of his home — because he stayed on the good side of his bosses.

Marvin drove a truck for a paper bag manufacturing company for over 10 years before he convinced his boss that the company's truck fleet was costing more than it was worth. Marvin proposed to buy all of the company's trucks on a contract and lease them back to the firm for less than they were paying to maintain the fleet. Marvin won the contract.

Soon, Standard Trucking Company was hauling all of the freight his former employer produced — plus other freight he picked up at other nearby warehouses. Marvin no longer drives trucks, but he travels a lot — to places like Hawaii, Europe and Australia. And, Marvin takes his efficiency awards to the bank every Friday afternoon

How to Specialize Your Way to Riches

There may be one part of your current job that is more profitable or enjoyable than the rest. You might be able to specialize in this task and earn a much better living than your present job offers.

Judy R. had worked as a reporter and editor on many weekly newspapers in the western states, but the job she enjoyed the most is the one that others like the least: proofreading. Today Judy offers a proofreading service to many publications in two states for a very lucrative fee, and she never has to leave home.

How to Find Profits in Interrelated Ventures

Thousands of people have found highly profitable businesses that can be operated at home by looking for services that are *similar* to their regular jobs.

Tito B. worked as a gardener for a large metropolitan landscaping firm. He enjoyed working in the out-of-doors, but preferred breeding and raising flowers to the monotonous work of cutting grass and trimming hedges that filled his nine-to-five job.

Three years ago, Tito started growing camellias and azaleas in a greenhouse at home. Today, Tito works for himself. He and his three employees raise these plants exclusively for his old bosses at the landscaping firm. Tito is making more money today than he ever did, because he found there was more profit — and more enjoyment — in a business related to his own job.

The best part about searching for a profitable business closely related to your present job is that you can use your experience and knowledge for your own profit instead of selling it to someone else for less than it's worth. You can also get a good deal of training in your chosen business completely paid for by your present employer.

So, don't burn your bridges behind you when you decide to strike out on your own in the world of wealth. You may be leaving some of your best — and most profitable — friends behind.

Millions are Waiting for You in Hobbies

No matter how much people gripe about inflation and taxes and the high cost of living, people have more "surplus money" today than ever before. They have more money to spend on hobbies and pleasure. In fact, coin collecting, stamp collecting and other well-known hobbies are billion-dollar-a-year industries where fortunes are being made almost every day. And, these smart fortune-hunters often never have to leave their home to find the path to wealth.

Art D. was a coin collector. He read, he studied and he learned everything he could find on numismatics. While still in high school, Art made lunch money by buying, selling and trading coins with other young collectors in the coin club he helped found.

Within a few months after graduation, Art had borrowed and saved enough money to open a small coin shop in a prime downtown location. In just a few short years, Art had a manager running his shop, while he flew back and forth across the nation buying and selling profitably at coin shows. Art was making well over $50,000 a year before his 21st birthday.

You, too, can quickly turn an enjoyable hobby or interest into a profitable full-time business by following these simple rules:

- Find out exactly what buyers in your field are buying.
- Search for the source with the lowest cost.
- Set up a quick and efficient marketing method.
- Buy only as much as you can resell at a handsome profit.

One of the most important rules of business is that if you learn how to buy right, you are half way to a profitable sale. To buy right you must know: (1) what you are buying and (2) its exact worth on today's market. Buying right means knowing as much as you can about your source *and* your customer. Remember:

A businessman is someone who buys something at 60 cents with hopes that someone will buy it from him for a dollar.

Your Past May Be the Most Profitable Way to Your Future

Very few people are working today in the trade they thought they would enter when they graduated from high school or college. People and society change. You may have studied to be an accountant, but today you're driving truck, or you may have been a mathematics major, who now sells shoes. But often, you still have an interest in getting back into the field in which you trained. You've thought about going back to school, learning more about your favorite subject and someday getting back into it.

Maybe a business of your own is your road toward that goal. You can start tomorrow, reading and studying in your spare time until your Profit Motivation discovers the right angle or combination that spells P-R-O-F-I-T in capital letters. A night school counselor or librarian can help you brush up on the rusty points, and you can soon be back on the right track toward your $50,000 a year job that can be handled from the comfort of your own home.

Your Friends Can Be Worth Millions

Another place to look for your profitable future is in your friends and acquaintances.

Have you ever talked with someone about jobs and found yourself saying, "Gee, I'd sure like to trade jobs with you. I could enjoy making a fortune doing that." Everyone has, and you just might be able to make that trade. The best part of this kind of fortune finding is that you can listen to your friend's "voice of experience" telling you exactly where the money is and how to avoid the mistakes that cost big profits.

If you have such a friend, plan right now to invite him or her over very soon for a session of education through Profit Motivation.

Thinking Your Way to Millions in Profit

There's another way to wealth. Brainstorming. It's easy, and it's highly profitable. All you need is a note pad, a pencil and a few hours of uninterrupted time.

You might call this: Designing A Better Mousetrap.

These are the things that you and I and every other consumer in the world is looking for. If you'll bring these things to us, we'll buy:

- Save us money on the necessities of life.
- Save us time and energy in the things we do.
- Offer us safety today and security tomorrow.
- Help us look and feel healthier and live longer.
- Offer us prestige and eminence.
- Give us comfort and peace of mind.
- Amuse and entertain us.

This is brainstorming — looking at the wants and needs of your fellow man and asking: (1) How can I offer him what he wants in return for a fair price and (2) How can I make a substantial profit by offering this service?

Sit down somewhere comfortable tonight, and relax your body and your mind. Open your inner mind to uncluttered thoughts, then probe your mind for a need around you and try to solve that need by asking yourself a few questions:

1. How strong is this need or problem?
2. How can I profitably fill this need?
3. How can I improve this service over someone else's?
4. What related needs can be filled for additional profits?

Just a few hours of Brainstorming each week can soon offer you dozens of ideas that may bring you an income of well over $50,000 a year — plus the independence of being your own boss.

THE MOST PROFITABLE BUSINESSES ARE ALSO THE EASIEST

There are basically six kinds of businesses. Some are much more profitable and make better home operations than others.

- Retail.
- Wholesale.
- Manufacturing.
- Research and Marketing.
- Consulting.
- Service.

A retail business usually demands that you have a store and lots of inventory in hopes that someone will walk through the door to buy from you at 40 percent above your cost. Although there are hundreds of thousands of retail businesses in the nation, they are not the most profitable enterprises to run and usually require quite a bit of money to start.

A wholesale business is sometimes better, because many of your variable expenses are eliminated and you can often earn a good profit with a wholesale business, though it may take many thousands of your own dollars plus thousands of borrowed dollars. Wholesaling is sometimes a good way to earn your *second* million, but not your first.

Manufacturing also has the drawback of needing cash for raw materials and inventory, but thousands of people are making their own pot of gold in their garage or spare bedroom with small-scale manufacturing. Don't overlook this type of business.

Research and marketing doesn't require an inventory, but it often requires high capital for promotion and publicity. A research and marketing firm develops ideas, either original ideas or in partnership with "thinkers," then uses its knowledge of business to try to find a buyer for the idea. A research and marketing firm may take the idea for a better mousetrap, find out if others have a patent on the idea, find out if someone is willing to buy the idea, then work out either an outright purchase of the idea or offer royalties on every mousetrap sold. This kind of business needs much less capital than the previous three and can often net the operator a higher profit.

Consulting is just that. Maybe you've built up a storehouse of knowledge on importing and exporting, or transportation problems, or house construction. You decide to turn this knowledge into profits and you specialize in your one field as a source for any information someone might need on the subject. You are a professional expert — no inventory, little capital outlay, high income and high profits.

Service businesses combine knowledge and equipment for substantial profits. Service businesses include janitorial services, catering services, phone answering services, contracting, dog grooming, remodeling, and a hundred other businesses that are both easy to get into and easy to operate out of your home.

As you can see, the most profitable businesses are those that can be operated from home with little capital investment for inventory and allow you to go looking for customers rather than waiting for them to come to you.

So, if you're looking for a highly profitable business that can offer you over $50,000 income a year while you work in your home, your best bet is a consulting service or a research and marketing service. Next best bets are service businesses and light manfacturing, with retail and wholesale businesses the least likely to offer you easy profits for the lowest initial investment.

HOW TO TEST YOUR IDEAS FOR PROFITABILITY

Now that you have a few ideas for profitable home businesses, let's test your best ideas for profitability before deciding on the one(s) that will carry you to riches.

Before you invest your own time and money into a business, you'll want to make sure it is the most profitable while offering the largest group of potential buyers. You can start your market research right now with a loose-leaf notebook. We'll call it your *Profitability Notebook*. Put dividers in it for each of the business ideas you've come up with, then fill each section with lots of notebook paper and you're ready to start answering a few basic profit questions about:

- Market potential.
- Market characteristics.
- Competition.
- Distribution methods.
- Profitability worksheet.
- Capital requirements.
- Related profits.

Let's take each point, one at a time, and answer a few important questions on your business ideas.

How to Test Market Potential

Market potential is the number of customers you might have for your business and service. If you plan on selling general products including gifts, gadgets and handicrafts, your potential market is the whole world. You can potentially sell your product or service to as many people as you can reach with your message. Just about everyone can use it.

But if you're selling a specialized product or service, like the buying and selling of oil rights in Idaho, your market potential is much smaller. Your market will primarily be oil speculators in Idaho.

So, the first question to answer in your new Profitability notebook is, "How many people might be potential customers for my business?" Often, the larger the market, the lower the price and profit margin. But, if you can mass produce and sell your product easily, you can make as big a fortune as the guy who sells only a few products at a profit of thousands of dollars each.

You'll also want to know how long your market will hold. Will there be a saturation point, where most of the people who want your product or service already have it? At this point of diminishing return, you may want to consider business diversification. You should be able to estimate market saturation after you decide (1) market size and (2) consumer lifespan of your product or service.

Go through each section of your Profitability Notebook answering these questions for each of your potential businesses:

- How large is the market for this product or service?
- Will there ever be a market saturation or will my business continue to be needed by past customers?

Find Out Who Your Customers Are

Evaluating market characteristics includes knowing what type of people will buy from you, why they buy and whether this kind of customer will continue to exist. To study market characteristics you can look for the answers to these questions:

- Is this business built on a quick-peaking fad or an overall inflationary growth?
- Can you expect this business to continue a few months, years, or a lifetime without a significant change in potential profits?
- Is the sale of this product or service dependent on local or industry pay days, or on seasonal purchases?
- Will people who buy from you today be in the market to buy from you again soon?
- Exactly what kind of people will be doing business with you — Average? Highly educated? Specialized industries? General public? Affluent? Men? Women?

Much of this information can be discovered by talking with the people who you feel are your potential customers. You can also find information on regional, ethnic and industrial economics from reference books available at most larger public and college libraries.

The more you know about your customer, the easier it is to sell him your product or service.

Stick Your Nose in Someone Else's Business

Sooner or later you're going to have to face competition in your field. Some businessmen fight their compeition like dogs. Others simply do the best job they can and let the competition worry about *them.*

The smartest businessman *profits* from his competition's mistakes.

With each of your potential business plans in mind, begin answering a few questions about your future competition:

- How successful are they?
- What is their estimated yearly gross income? Profit?
- How can you offer their customers a better product or service and still maintain a good profit margin?
- What type of advertising and promotion do they do?
- What business mistakes are they making that you could capitalize on?
- What additional services could you offer that your potential competition does not?

A little economic sleuthing will save you thousands of dollars in market research and help you learn more about the kind of business that will take you toward your wealth goals.

Distribution Is Half of the Sale

There are many ways you can distribute your product or service: by mail, freight, phone, in person, through sales agents, wholesalers, jobbers and more. You can find out the best way to take your business to your customer by asking:

- What is the most economical method of distribution for my business?
- Which is the fastest?
- Which method is the most profitable?
- Should I try to do all of my own selling or should I have someone else do it for me on commission?

- How can I develop the best distribution system?
- What back-up system can I use in case of emergency?

In many service-related businesses, distribution of your finished product is no problem, but in some home-operated businesses, your distribution method can spell the difference between a small and a highly profitable business.

How to Develop a Profitability Worksheet

Charity begins at home, but not in a home business. You are building your business in order to make a high profit on your knowledge and ability. So, you must clearly understand all of the costs involved in offering your product or service to buyers and know how much you should get for it in order to earn this profit.

Your Profitability Notebook should have the answers to these questions for each of the businesses you are considering:

- What type of equipment or machinery will I need for my business, and how much will each item cost?
- Can I buy these assets at a dealer discount or in used condition at a lower price?
- How much will maintenance of these units cost?
- Do I have enough room in my home for current office needs? Future expansion?
- What amount of overhead expenses (lights, heat, taxes, supplies) should I expect to pay? What percentage of my expected income?
- What tax advantages can I take advantage of as a home-operated business?
- How much will each unit (or each hour) cost me to produce?
- How many of these units or hours will I need to sell to reach my economic goals in three months? Six months? A year? Five years?
- What percentage of my initial investment (time and money) can I expect to earn?
- What methods and sources can I use to increase business when I want to?

A simplified course in bookkeeping-accounting will tell you that assets less liabilities equals capital; what you own less what you owe equals what you're worth. Profit is everything you have left from your income after you've paid all of your expenses.

So, to increase your profits you simply have to increase your income without a corresponding increase in expenses. If you are in a service business where you are selling your time and talents, your overhead expenses (office and related costs) stay pretty much the same as your income grows. Thus, more income with the same expenses equals higher profits. Your goal is to (1) get business and (2) get *more* business.

Your Profitability Worksheet should estimate what assets (desk, typewriter, cash, merchandise, machines) you will need, while it lists your probable liabilities (business loans, money owed to office supply company and so on). It should also estimate projected income from your potential businesses per week, per month and per year as well as the expenses you expect to have in earning this income.

Put everything down on paper. Not only for yourself, but also for your banker or backer. He'll want to know exactly how you expect to pay him back with interest.

How to Estimate Capital Requirements
Next, you have to decide just how much money you're going to need to start your business. In the case of a service business run from a desk in one room of your home, the money you'll need will be small unless you plan a heavy advertising and promotion campaign. If you're thinking of repairing televisions or other appliances in your garage, the capital requirements for equipment and tools could run a few thousands dollars. Some types of businesses, especially those needing a large inventory, will need quite a bit of capital to start.

How are you going to get this money? Some of it can come from your own savings, but the best way to start is with rented money. That's right. You can rent or borrow thousands of dollars on your signature or with some collateral at from eight to 18 percent interest so why not borrow money, make a 25 to 2500 percent profit and pocket the difference.

SIMILARITY BREEDS PROFITS

Before you finally decide on which of your potential business ventures you want to find your fortune in, look at whether the field is a busy thoroughfare with highly profitable ideas all around or a dead-end street with only one or two profitable ventures available.

For instance, you've decided to install burglar alarm systems. You could easily branch out into smoke detectors, fire alarms, locksmithing, electrical contracting, security patrol, intercom systems, electronics and more.

Test your ideas for profitability and save yourself thousands of dollars in "professional" market studies that often won't tell you more than you could easily learn yourself.

THREE WAYS TO RESEARCH YOUR PROFIT IDEAS

There are three things you can begin to do this week that will help you decide which of these potential businesses is the best and most profitable for you:

1. Talk with potential customers.
2. Talk to similar businessmen.
3. Get a job.

Listen to Your Customers

Who can better tell you the value of your product than your future customers? By talking with a few of them, you may find out both what they want from your business and what they are willing to pay. Best of all, you may be able to line up advance contracts for your business to help you on the road to higher profits.

Make a list of at least a dozen potential users and interview each of them on what they expect in using your product or service. Let them do the talking. Don't tell them too much about your plans in advance, though. Magicians are no fun after you know how the trick is done.

Learn from the Pioneers

Someone, somewhere, is probably running a business just like the one you want to run from your home. The trick is to find him and coax information from him on how to start, how to find customers, how to operate at the highest profit, and how to handle taxes.

Every businessman I've ever met loves to talk about his business — if he doesn't feel he is giving away information that may cost him customers from a dishonest competitor. In your market research of profitable ventures, you'll find many people in similar businesses who won't mind offering help in confidence.

These people can be your business's biggest assets.

Make Money While Your Learn

Then there is the "hands on" method of profit search. If you're not now in the business you are looking to start, you may want to consider a part or full-time job in it to learn as much as you can from the inside. You may decide to work evenings or weekends for a few months to learn as much as you can about costs, customers, capital and credit. You may only make a few dollars an hour at your temporary job, but the education you'll get will be worth thousands of dollars in future profits.

As your eyes begin to see with Profit Motivation, you will soon view the millions of dollars in easy-to-reach profits that surround you each and every day. Profit, like beauty, is everywhere. All you have to do to enjoy it is open your eyes and your mind.

THINGS YOU CAN DO NOW

Our lesson on the tactics of profit search is over. Now it's time for the homework. If you do it well, you'll receive something much better than a good grade. You'll find the wealth and happiness you justly deserve.

1. Start your Profitability Notebook right now, and list profitable ventures that you could develop from knowledge of your regular job, related jobs, hobbies and interests, previous training, friends and acquaintances, popular fads or general brainstorming.

2. Choose the five most profitable ideas that appeal to you and start a section of your notebook for each.

3. Begin looking at each of your profit ventures for potential, market characteristics, competition, distribution methods, profitability, capital needed and related profits available.

4. Talk with potential customers and selected businessmen about your ventures to find out what they want and how you can get their business. You might also consider getting a part or full-time job in the field if you are not already in it.

5. Think Profit Motivation

5

Dollar Dynamics
Can
Work for You

Fact: Your financial success depends on the number of opportunities you recognize and use to your own benefit.

This chapter will show you how to use the Power of Dollar Dynamics to locate the most profitable opportunity available to you—and will outline two dozen highly successful business ideas.

THE DOLLAR DYNAMICS SYSTEM OF WEALTH-BUILDING POWER

Money moves mountains.

It's an old phrase, but it's true. Why?

It holds true because people recognize what money is and does. Everyone, from the small boy with a paper route to the successful corporate executive, knows that, in ample quantity, money can be freely exchanged for nearly anything he or she wants in this purchasable world. They all realize that money isn't everything, but it is a clever way of keeping score.

The Power of Dollar Dynamics uses this attraction that money has to create opportunities that can be turned into high profits. Dollar Dynamics can help you see opportunities for what they really are—prospects for advancement. Dollar Dynamics can motivate you to thoroughly test each opportunity you see to discover its own value. Dollar Dynamics can motivate your customers to spend more money with you in order to save or earn money. The Power of Dollar Dynamics can be harnessed and used to build your own personal fortune. It's a Power that can breed more power.

How Clayton B. Used Dollar Dynamics on His Way to the Top

Clayton B. understood the Power of Dollar Dynamics. His hobby was inventing gadgets. Most of his inventions were of little profit value—until he came up with one that would not only open a can easily, but would also serve as a sealable pouring spout. Clayton knew that they could be made in quantity for less than 15 cents each and sell for more than a dollar.

Clayton lacked the money to put his combination can opener-pouring spout into production and distribution—but he did know about the Power of Dollar Dynamics.

The first thing Clayton did was develop a market study on his proposed gadget. He found out exactly how much they would cost to manufacture, what price they would sell best at, how they could be distributed inexpensively, and—most important—where he might get backing for such a business venture.

After further study, Clayton took his facts and ideas to the first financier on his list. Clayton told him exactly what it would cost to begin his proposed business, how much profit was involved, what expenses were and how much interest he could pay on a loan. Clayton came prepared with the Power of Dollar Dynamics. Clayton showed the financier how he could profit from this opportunity. He motivated the financier to agree to back Clayton with $80,000—because Clayton showed him how his dollars could bring him more dollars.

Clayton didn't stop there. He continued using the Power of Dollar Dynamics to obtain credit from suppliers, to find and develop a profit-motivated sales force and to eventually motivate retailers into buying his product to resell it "at a healthy profit."

Clayton fully understood that Dollar Dynamics changes opportunities into profit-making ventures. He knew that *the Power of Dollar Dynamics is the power of the dollar to bring you more dollars.*

Today, Clayton's salary is over $110,000 a year as chairman of the board of his own manufacturing firm. His duties include being a consultant and attending the yearly board meeting. Clayton somehow finds other things to do during the rest of the year.

THE DOLLAR DYNAMICS SYSTEM OF OPPORTUNITY DEVELOPMENT

As you study the concepts of Profit Motivation and Dollar Dynamics, you'll begin seeing more and more opportunities that can be made highly profitable with the skills you now have. How can you find the best opportunities for you?

Each opportunity must eventually be judged by only one thing—how it fits *your* needs and *your* abilities. If the opportunity isn't right for you, it isn't right. But don't give up.

There are plenty of excellent opportunities waiting for you *if* you learn to recognize them.

The Dollar Dynamics System of Opportunity Development is:

- Know your financial goals.
- Be aware of your skills.
- Count your resources.
- Look for opportunity everywhere.
- Estimate potential for each opportunity.
- Analyze your Opportunity Ratio.
- Choose the most Dollar Dynamic opportunity.

Know Your Financial Goals

This should be the easiest step for you in the Dollar Dynamic System of Opportunity Development, because you have already established your long- and short-range financial goals. You know how much money you want to earn, and you know how long it should take to earn it. Best of all, you are starting to look at a few of the ways you can get there—opportunities—and are beginning to see some of them as better than others.

Make sure that these goals are not only on your Wealth Worksheet but also in your mind. Remind yourself of the specific financial goals you have set for yourself, the things you expect to receive when you reach those goals. Take a moment to motivate yourself with the vision of your new home, car, boat, workshop, hobby or whatever you have promised yourself when you "arrive." Keep your financial goals firmly fixed in your mind, and see yourself enjoying their benefits.

Be Aware of Your Skills

Your Skills Worksheet, developed in Chapter 3, will prepare you for your opportunities in a unique way. It will

outline not only your current skills, but will also point out
the skills you can develop to bring you wealth.

Check your Skills Worksheet for those skills that you
know are most profitable and underline them. Remember
them as the most likely roads to your goals.

Count Your Resources

What resources do you have that can help you develop
opportunities into profits?

- Time.
- Money.

To take stock of your resources, estimate the amount of
time you will be able to offer to a worthwhile opportunity.
How many hours a day? A week? A month? Also, estimate
the financial investment that you are willing to put into an
opportunity if it shows promise of Dollar Dynamics, the
power of the dollar to bring you more dollars. What could
your initial investment be? Could you add to that investment
on a weekly or monthly basis? How much?

Count your resources right now. They can both add up
and multiply.

Look for Opportunity Everywhere

As Chapter 4 suggests, opportunity is everywhere: at
home, in your job, in hobbies, in friends, in education, in
day-to-day activities. Use the Power of Profit Motivation
and the Power of Dollar Dynamics to open your eyes to the
hundreds of opportunities around you every day. The best
way to insure the most profitable and enjoyable opportunity
is to gather the best opportunity from the widest field. Start
today, looking at everything you do for that new idea, that
small change, that improvement that can make you
wealthier than your dreams.

Estimate the Potential of Each Opportunity

Estimating your profit for each opportunity you study is much easier than it might seem. Initially, you aren't looking for the exact amount of dollars and cents you'll make in the first year. For now, you are interested in whether this enterprise can give you approximately enough to reach the financial goals you've set for yourself.

Your Profitability Worksheet, from Chapter 4, will help you decide whether the enterprise is lucrative enough to meet your goals or not. If not, forget it. There will be enough enterprises that *will* meet your standards to allow you to turn down the less profitable ones.

Analyze the Opportunity Ratio

Here's how to rate an opportunity, based on how much income it can offer and how much risk is involved. Ramsey's Opportunity Ratio is:

$$O = I \times R$$

Or, *Opportunity is equal to the Income multiplied by the Risk.* Use the Income, Risk and Opportunity Scales on page 000 to analyze your opportunity. An "I" of 8 is an income of approximately 80 percent of your financial goal. An "I" of 3 is only 30 percent. An "R" of 8 is a low risk in which your capital is secured with equipment and merchandise that can be easily resold for little or no loss. An "R" of 2 is a very high risk.

Multiply the Income rating by the Risk rating and you have a relative Opportunity Ratio that will help you in comparing opportunities. The higher the "O", the better the opportunity.

Choose the Most Dynamic Opportunity

Decision time.

Once you have the facts in front of you, it's time to study them and decide on the best opportunity for you. You know your own financial goals; you are aware of your potential and marketable skills; you have counted your current resources of time and money; you have looked for opportunity all around you; you have estimated the potential; and you have found, from a review of all these factors, an Opportunity Ratio for the enterprises you are considering.

You can decide on the best opportunity for you by following these four Dollar Dynamic Decision steps:

- Eliminate the least likely.
- Choose the best of the remaining opportunities.
- Check the opportunity thoroughly.
- Move into action.

From your field of a dozen or more potential money making opportunities, you can easily eliminate a third of them for these reasons:

- Income potential is too low.
- Risk factor is too high for income potential.
- Too much initial capital is needed.
- You have little interest or motivation in the opportunity.

It's an easier step to choose one outstanding opportunity from those remaining. You can do it by eliminating some wealth ventures and combining others. Once you've chosen one opportunity or group of opportunities that you think will take you to your goal, begin your profitability study again, looking closer at how much profit, risk and initial capital are involved. Pin your estimates of costs and income closer.

Then it's time to *act*. You've penciled figures, you've scratched your head, you've eliminated ideas that weren't "just right" for you. It's time to take the best opportunity you've found and start building it into the highly profitable and enjoyable business venture that you are sure can take you to your financial goals.

DOLLAR DYNAMIC BUSINESS IDEAS

Here are two dozen proven business ideas that have a potential of at least $50,000 income a year and that can be easily operated out of your own home or garage. Add these to the many operating businesses outlined in other chapters of this book, and you have nearly 100 money-making opportunities that use the Power of Dollar Dynamics.

Going into Business with Uncle Sam

Whether you like it or not, Uncle Sam is your partner in business. He's always there, watching over your shoulder as you count your income and—just as sure as the tax man—he has his hand out for his share of the profits. So why not get some of that money back by using many of the services that he offers to businessmen.

The biggest service you can use is the mail service. Uncle will take your message by truck, plane and foot over more than 3,000 miles for less than the cost of a package of gum. Make money with this service. Find customers, offer them your merchandise or service, deliver it to them and receive their money, all by mail. Here are some of the mail-order businesses you can operate with little capital outlay from the comfort of your own home:

Import-export: Millions of dollars cross the oceans and continents each day in one of the most lucrative mail-order businesses ever conceived—international trade by mail. Goods are imported and exported to and from nearly every country in the free world. It's a highly profitable business.

Top wealth opportunities are found in this field of business. Does your present employer handle a product or service that you could export? Does he need a product that can be easily imported? You may even find a product or gadget in one of the hundreds of import trade catalogs that you would enjoy importing and selling for a lucrative profit.

Your wealth-building import-export business can begin with little more than a desk and typewriter in your home, stamps and envelopes, and a book or mail-order course on the import-export business. The classified sections of many newsstand magazines will offer many addresses of firms that offer further information on one of the easiest and richest Dollar Dynamic enterprises ever developed.

Domestic merchandise: Other people are building their fortunes by making or reselling merchandise by mail to customers here in the United States which involves less paperwork, less mailing costs and less time.

You could sell wood carvings you make at home, or handicraft kits, or novelty items or one of a thousand other things that are found in mail circulars and catalogs delivered to your door every year. Anything that can be sold, can be sold by mail.

To research this lucrative field for profitability, get on as many mail-order merchandise mailing lists as possible. Find out what's for sale and by whom. Look for ways you can offer similar merchandise better, quicker or less expensively than others. Look for unique products that can be bought and sold profitably by mail from a business at home.

Many mail order businesses began with nothing more than a good idea, a few letterheads and stamps, and the U.S. Mail. Yet, hundreds of these "quiet businesses" report gross sales of over $1 million a year. There's always room for one more.

Bookstore: Just about everyone reads books, and there are over one hundred specialized book clubs in the nation. They cover every special interest from coin collecting to electronics, from needlepoint to child care, from archeology to model planes. And, other clubs service people who like to read category fiction such as mysteries, gothic romances and science fiction novels.

Don L. started the Paperback Book Exchange in 1967. Don was an avid reader who would sometimes consume half a dozen paperbacks in a week. His pastime not only got expensive, but Don was running out of titles available in his small town. His wealth idea was to have people exchange paperbacks by mail. They send him five paperbacks and one dollar plus postage and he sends them five different paperbacks. Don's profit is a neat $1 per package for just typing new address labels and sending the packages back out. Don doesn't devote full time to his wealth venture. He still reads a lot, but Don also earns a full-time wage from a profitable business that grew out of a need.

Publishing: Others publish their own books for profit. One such enterprise, Jude Publications, sold a booklet listing over 200 things that can be ordered through the mail free of charge: books, samples, information. The booklet sold for a dollar through national magazines, but cost only 12 ½ cents to produce.

You can publish small booklets on nearly any subject in the world. People will always want to know how to do something better, quicker, more profitably, easier, longer or more enjoyably. A typewriter and a local quick-print shop may put you into the mail-order publishing business. A husband-and-wife business, Jude Publications started with a borrowed typewriter and $200 in cash: $125 for printing 1,000 booklets and $75 for initial advertising and postage costs. The $200 soon grew into $1,000, which grew into larger publishing enterprises eventually valued at over $20,000.

Correspondence school: Do you have a skill or trade that you could teach to others by written instruction?. If so, you can earn high profits with your own correspondence school.

Mrs. Dorothy T. was a seamstress whose work was always in demand. She wanted to retire, but felt she couldn't afford to quit. After seeing a few correspondence school ads in magazines she decided to try to write her own course in home sewing. Friends loved it, and people who heard about it wanted copies. Before long, Dorothy was mimeographing lessons and selling sets by word-of-mouth at five dollars a lesson.

A business consultant helped Mrs. T. set up the mechanics of a correspondence school in a spare bedroom of her home. Today, Mrs. T. spends 10 hours a week with her business, in which she earns more than twice the salary she made in 40 hours a week as a seamstress.

You can set up your own correspondence school by answering all of the ads for other schools you see, studying their sales literature and samples and then designing your own set of lessons and pricing them below others. Dozens of individuals are now making over $50,000 a year at home with correspondence schools on welding, auto body repair, mail-order enterprise, accounting, real estate, law, truck driving, broadcasting, electronics, and other fields. Many of them started with under $200 in initial capital. The field—and the profits—are wide open.

Mailing service: People want letters and packages mailed from other cities for many reasons. They may want to write to someone without letting them know where they live. They may want to use a big city address for a business that is actually in a small town.

You can cash in on these needs by offering a remail service. It starts by placing an ad in various publications that offers to remail letters from your city for postage plus 25 cents. The only cost to you is your ad, which might read:

> REMAILS: 25¢ plus postage
> Box XXX
> Los Angeles, CA 98765.

Other profitable mailing services including stuffing envelopes, addressing envelopes, mimeographing, printing broker and mailing list broker. Each has the advantage of requiring little or no starting capital while offering the potential of high earnings at home.

18 Other Profitable Home-Operated Businesses

Vending route: Thousands of high-profit vending companies are operated from desks in homes across the nation. Their owners may travel the countryside servicing machines located in taverns, gas stations and shopping centers, but they call their home the "home office."

You can start your own vending company in one of two ways: (1) Buy an established route or (2) Start your own route with leased or purchased equipment. The most profitable vending companies specialize in one type of machine at first: food, amusement or merchandise vendors. Later they expand as their capital expands. If you have small investment capital and a solid goal, vending suppliers will often offer equipment on credit to allow you to set up more profitable vending machines than you could with just your own capital.

Talk with non-competing vending route operators before you decide. Read the "Business Opportunities" ads in your metropolitan paper. Check the phone book for vending route suppliers. They can all offer you profitable insight into the problems and rewards of a very lucrative home-operated business.

Buy and sell antiques: Bill and Dotty A. love antiques. They used to spend nearly every weekend scouring the countryside for hidden relics, for fun rather than profit. Then Bill, at 57, was laid off his job. Together, they decided to use part of their savings to start an antique business.

Bill is now 61 and can retire wealthy any day he wishes, but he's having too much fun to stop. Bill and Dotty own a motor home with a trailer in which they travel three Northwestern states, buying and selling antiques. They may stop along the way for a week or two and enjoy visiting the sites before they get down to the business of antiques. In two more years, they plan to choose their favorite town, buy an old house near the downtown area and set up a more permanent antique shop and home. But right now, they are enjoying life too much to pull off the road.

You can do the same. Some antique dealers specialize in historic eras or geographic areas, while others specialize in certain types of memorabilia. Beginning capital requires only a few good antiques—which can be sold on consignment—and the cost of handbills and business cards. Bill and Dotty's income is only $22,000 a year, but other dealers working from a Main Street store often ring up $50,000, $60,000 and more in profits each year.

Sell coins and stamps: Numismatics and philately are both highly profitable hobbies that can be turned into businesses with a potential of over $50,000 a year at home. Some coin and stamp dealers reserve one room of their home as a showcase for other collectors to view at their own convenience. The word gets around to other collectors quickly and—if prices are right and trades can be made—a reputable dealer can earn a very comfortable living without having to leave home.

If coin and stamp dealing appeals to you, read the hobby publications for both profitable developments and advertisements from potential competitors. They will give you clear ideas on how to merchandise and price your product. Your initial inventory could be a good selection of a certain type of coin or stamp rather than a little bit of everything. You may be able to gather much of it from other collectors, to be sold on consignment, and you could then promote your new hobby business through local clubs and shows. Coin and stamp dealing can be a low-capital high-profit business that can offer you an income of over $50,000 a year from your own home.

Art and frame gallery: Art is very big—and very profitable. There are thousands of amateur and professional artists today trying to sell their work—and even more people interested in buying art in every style and price range. Bring the two together and you can make a fortune without leaving home.

Linda Y. was bored. She enjoyed staying home, but she also wanted to meet new people. The most outgoing of an otherwise quiet and artistic family, Linda struck on an idea for a new business one day that would break her boredom, give her more money to spend and bring new faces to her home—an art gallery. Linda started her gallery by getting her artistic brother, Mark, to paint a sign on a pallette which she hung below her mailbox. It read: "Linda's Art Gallery." She then asked other painters in her family and in a group of friends if they would like to hang their paintings in her home to be sold on a commission basis. Nearly every one contributed a painting.

Soon, Linda's front room and dining room *looked* like an art gallery. The sign near the mailbox and a small ad and story in the local newspaper brought area art collectors to Linda's home. The collectors brought money. Soon, Linda was selling frames that her husband made on weekends in the garage and the whole family was involved in her new business venture. Linda's portion of sales comes to nearly $1,300 every month.

If you have an interest in art or frames, think about ways you can apply this highly profitable home business to your own needs. Expanded, this one idea could take you beyond your goal of $50,000 a year from your own home.

Workshop projects: Linda's husband, Rick, loved to work in his garage workshop—a welcome change from his job as a cost accountant. When Linda opened her art gallery, Rick struck on the idea of making frames, finishing them and selling them with the paintings. One weekend netted four frames, which were then hung on the wall. *All four sold by the following weekend*—so Rick got back in the shop and produced half a dozen more. Rick now makes six to ten frames on Saturday, and they usually sell by the next weekend. He's doing some cost accounting—to see if he can make a full-time living in his shop. With the help of Linda's art gallery, he just might be able to.

Other profitable workshop projects include small windmills, planters, lawn and patio furniture, prefab doghouses, plywood cutouts for exterior decoration and ornamental shutters. A review of workshop books and magazines will net a number of profitable workshop projects that can be started with minimum capital in your home.

Raising animals or cash crops: If you have any amount of land, from a 50 by 100 foot house lot to a 20 acre parcel, you can turn it into cash by raising small animals or cash crops for resale.

John and Winnie T. just bought a place in the country. They were new to country life, but with the help of a few books, John started a small herb garden and Winnie began raising pheasants for show. They now make more than enough from their part-time enterprises to keep up the payments on their spacious country home.

Capital requirements for these businesses are low if you don't count the cost of the land. Seeds and young stock can be purchased with less than $100. A small start will tell you in one season whether you'll want to expand your business into a high-profit venture. Books are available at libraries and county extension offices on both small-animal raising and small-scale farming.

Animal care and training: If one of your skills is the ability to work well with animals, look at the profits available in animal care.

Businesses based on skills with animals include raising pedigree dogs, cats or other animals, breaking and training horses, raising animals for show and dog- and cat-sitting.

Your own natural talents plus supplementary information from animal care books and magazines can offer you a wealth of business opportunities that can be profitably run from your home. Many of them can be expanded to offer you your wealth goal within a couple of years.

Car repair: The average car owner is constantly looking for someone he can trust for honest car repair at a reasonable price. If you can fill that need, you can find huge profits without leaving home.

Carl D. began tuning up cars for friends on the weekends. Soon, his weekends were full because he did quality work at a low price and guaranteed everything he did. He soon expanded his part-time business by taking his tools to the large mill where he worked, repairing cars for employees working other shifts. He saved his customers both money and time, and they rewarded him by bringing him so much business that within six months he was forced to quit his shift work at the mill and devote his full time to his auto repair business—and give himself a five dollar an hour raise.

You can do the same thing. Your only requirements are collecting the tools you need and brushing up on auto repair techniques. Promise yourself and your customers honest work at a fair price and let your satisfied customers do your advertising. Many self-employed auto mechanics make $50,000 a year and more from their garage at home.

Bookkeeping and tax service: Florence M. started small, too. She had done tax filings for her friends for half a dozen years before one of them asked her to do the bookkeeping for their business. Florence then decided to make a business of it and opened a room of her house as "The Home Office," offering a bookkeeping and tax service, a resume and typing service, mimeographing and other related services.

Florence now employs her 19-year-old daughter to help with the bookkeeping and typing, and her business profits now exceed the checks her husband brings home each week.

Your bookkeeping and tax service business can be started with minimum capital if you have a desk, typewriter and extra space in your home. If you lack the necessary skills or need to brush up, there are dozens of courses available from correspondence schools and local colleges that can help insure your success. Before you open for business, talk with the owner of a similar service in a noncompeting area and you will find a wealth of business information worth thousands of dollars to your new enterprise.

Construction contractor: If you have a working knowledge of the building trade, you may be able to build a contracting business at home. Contractors oversee the construction of homes, apartments, office buildings and shopping centers. They "let" bids out to subcontractors to do the physical work such as plumbing, electrical work, drywall, roofing, painting, and are responsible for the unit being finished on time and within a certain price range. For his services, the contractor usually receives 15 percent of the cost of the building being constructed. That's $7,500 on a $50,000 home.

Being a construction contractor takes special knowledge and ability, but if you have those assets on your Skills Worksheet, you can earn an impressive salary from your office at home.

Property investment and management: Richard S. was a moderately successful real estate salesman for three years before he accidently struck his gold mine. Richard had sold a home for a local businessman who was so happy with the sale and proceeds that he asked Richard to list his business property. The price tag was $250,000.

Richard didn't know where to start. He talked with his broker to find the best method of marketing the property. The broker suggested contacting all the businessmen in the area with similar businesses to see if they wished to expand. That afternoon Richard made nearly a dozen calls.

The next morning he had three appointments to show the property, and the same afternoon, one of the businessmen made a full-price offer which was accepted by a very surprised seller.

Richard was so busy that he hadn't stopped to figure his commission on the sale until after the deal was closed. He gasped when he got the check: half of 10 percent commission on a $250,000 sale is $12,500. Not bad for two days work.

Richard repeated the process on another commercial property just to prove to himself that it wasn't a fluke and then made up his mind to specialize in listing and selling commercial properties. Today Richard owns his own brokerage firm and keeps the entire 10 percent commission. He runs his commercial property firm from one large room in his new $125,000 home.

If salesmanship, business experience or real estate are listed on your Skills Worksheet, look into operating your own property investment and management firm. Initial capital is low, and profits are high.

Rental agency: A highly profitable business that has developed in the last decade is the rental agency. Everyone sometimes needs something that is too expensive to buy to use just once. Also, everyone has something that others might want to borrow and use once in awhile. These two facts opened up a profitable business idea for two men.

Larry S. and Don A. are back-fence neighbors who often traded tools and equipment. Together, they now operate "The Back-Fence Rental Agency" from an attic room with a desk, phone and card file in Don's house. The card file contains information on just about anything available on today's market costing over $20. It shows the owner's name and how he or she can be contacted to rent the item.

The idea is simple. Someone wants to use an item for an hour, day, week or month, but doesn't feel they want to buy it. They call up "The Back-Fence Rental Agency," find out who has one for rent and how much the owners will charge. The Back-Fence Rental Agency receives 25 percent of the rental fee for the referral.

Other rental agencies specialize in recreational vehicles, garden tools and equipment, painting equipment, earth-moving equipment and commercial house-cleaning equipment. Check the market to see if you can find the need for a profitable rental agency that can earn you high profits from your home.

Employment agency: The same can be done with people. An employment agency can be set up in your home to match the employer and the potential employee with a simple card filing system. Fees range from a flat $10 to $100 per successful referral to half of the first month's wages. Your fee can be paid by either the employer or job seeker.

Travel bureau: Today's travel bureau is very sophisticated and usually has a half-dozen employees, a computer link-up with airports and hotels, and an expensive downtown office. You can operate your own travel bureau from your own home by *specializing.* Your clients can be members of a certain fraternity or lodge, office complex, factory or trade. You can specialize in low-cost trips to the Orient, Mexico, Canada or Alaska. You can also specialize in rail, bus or other travel.

If you lack experience in the travel field but are interested in this enterprise, you can do one of these things: Take a part or full-time job in a travel agency as a trainee; take a correspondence or business school course in travel agency work; study one type of travel, start your business, then expand as your knowledge expands.

If you enjoy people and are interested in the wide field of world travel you can earn a 15 percent commission and other high profits by operating a travel agency from your own home.

Advertising — public relations: Hundreds of small advertising and public relations firms are operating from homes across the nation. An advertising firm sells a service rather than a product, so fancy store windows on Main Street are unnecessary. All that is necessary is a knowledge of advertising methods, buying and public relations. If these are among your skills, look further into this business opportunity, which usually offers from 15 percent to as much as 30 percent commission for advertising and high hourly fees for public relations work. Start-up overhead is low, since all you need is a desk, a typewriter and a phone. And, many self-employed ad agency owners earn $50,000, $60,000 and even $75,000 a year from their home offices.

Sales agency: If you are a good salesperson, you can operate a sales agency from your own home and earn well over $50,000 income a year.

Jack C. was one of the best vacuum-cleaner salesmen in his state, but he wanted to slow down and take it easier. He was getting tired of walking house to house in strange cities, living out of motel rooms and eating in restaurants.

One day, Jack hit upon an idea: Why not sell vacuums by phone? Jack spent that evening in his motel room, sketching out a plan that would bring him more income than he was then making, while letting him work from an office at home. By using a city directory, Jack could establish income levels and learn how long homeowners had lived at their current address. He could qualify their ability to pay without ever seeing or talking with them. Jack decided to start selling vacuums by phone to people who made over $20,000 a year and who had lived at their current address three years or more. He could sell them deluxe vacuums.

Jack's sales approach was to call them and offer to send them a vacuum cleaner on a free ten-day home trial. As he talked with them on the phone, he would "qualify" them to establish whether they were truly in the market for a vacuum and whether they could afford to purchase it. If they passed both qualifications, Jack took a calculated gamble and sent them a deluxe vacuum cleaner by bus express. He found when the package was expected to arrive at the customer's home and called soon afterwards to answer questions and offer a few tips on its use over the phone.

Three days later, a contract was sent by registered mail, and Jack called again. Jack found that his success ratio by this method was over 80 percent. His phone bill, freight bill and postage expenses were high, but were actually lower per unit sold than his travel time and the expenses of his old method of door-to-door sales.

Jack is still the highest producer in his state, but he now gets a game of golf in on sunny days and reads a lot on cooler days. Jack earned $63,00 last year—without leaving home.

Credit and collection: Another easy method of earning a high income with a phone is a credit and collection agency. The concept is that businesses give you their bad debts to collect and offer you 50 percent of everything collected. Successful collection agencies have one to six employees who make telephone calls to overdue accounts and use a standard "pitch" or sales talk to debtors encouraging them to pay past-due bills. This is usually followed up with a letter, explaining that legal action will be taken if the bill is not paid within a certain number of days. The final step, if profitable, is to take larger debtors to court to pay what they owe.

Some collection agencies are abusive, but most are responsible businesses who legally insist that debtors pay their bills. Profits are large; costs are low. Employees are often paid a commission on what is collected. If this is a business that appeals to you, be aware that hundreds of collection agencies earn their owners handsome five- and even six-figure salaries.

Consulting service: Our final business opportunity is the most general and can be operated by anyone with a good knowledge of nearly any subject or occupation. Profitable consulting services include business investments, efficient homemaking, credit, business management, education, travel, printing, publishing, consumerism, hobbies, labor relations and dozens of others. Consultants often charge $15 to $50 an hour to tell people how they can do something more efficiently or profitably.

Alvin M. was a millwright for over 20 years before he started his own consulting firm. With little more than a few business cards—and his knowledge and experience—Alvin began a business that now offers him $40 an hour plus travel expenses for advising paper and aluminum mills of the best methods of installing new and used equipment in their mills. His home is his office, but the world has been his factory. Alvin has helped with installations in most parts of the U.S., plus New Zealand, Taiwan, England and Saudi Arabia.

And Alvin enjoys every minute of it.

The dollar has the power to make *more* dollars when you combine the Power of Dollar Dynamics and creative ideas for profitable enterprises that can be developed with the skills you have today.

RAMSEY'S OPPORTUNITY RATIO

$$O = I \times R$$

INCOME FACTOR	RISK FACTOR
10 — 100% of income goal	10 — no risk
9 — 90% of income goal	9 — minimal risk
8 — 80% of income goal	8 — low risk
7 — 70% of income goal	7 — low-to-moderate risk

6 —	60% of income goal	6 —	moderate risk
5 —	50% of income goal	5 —	average risk
4 —	40% of income goal	4 —	above average risk
3 —	30% of income goal	3 —	high risk
2 —	20% of income goal	2 —	very high risk
1 —	10% of income goal	1 —	extremely high risk

THINGS YOU CAN DO NOW

Make the Power of Dollar Dynamics work for you. Turn the power of the dollar to make more dollars into a profit-making machine that will take you to your financial goals—and beyond—by doing these things *right now:*

1. **Develop your Power of Dollar Dynamics.** Put your mind to work full time in searching for opportunities that will bring you wealth.

2. **Look for the best opportunity.** Estimate the potential of each opportunity you see with my Opportunity Ratio. Narrow down the field to the most profitable wealth venture for you. (Chapter 6 will show you how to specialize each venture for higher profits.)

3. **Study successful businesses.** Review the two dozen profitable business ideas in this chapter for opportunities that you can apply.

4. **Choose your general wealth venture.** Decide on the basic type of business you are most interested in developing into your $50,000 a year business-at-home.

5. **Think Profit Motivation.**

6
Mastermind Your Way to Riches

In the last three chapters, you've learned how to:

- Set your GOALS.
- ORGANIZE your search.
- LOCATE the right opportunity.

This chapter will show you, step-by-step, how to develop your opportunities into riches by research and marketing of your Profit-Motivated enterprise. You will learn how to Mastermind your way to riches.

HOW TO MAKE LUCK HAPPEN TO YOU

Can you imagine standing before a fireplace and saying, "Give me some heat and I'll give you a log." It sounds ridiculous, doesn't it? But that's what many otherwise-enterprising people try to do. They want something before they have given something. And, just like the fireplace, opportunity waits for them to make the first move. Should they blame the fireplace for not giving them the heat they wanted? Or should they first decide what the fireplace wants—and get it—before expecting to receive what they want?

Taking advantage of money-making opportunities isn't much different. If you want people to bring you the riches, you must first offer them something they need and want. You must serve them before they will serve you. Call it the "Law of Cause and Effect" or the "Golden Rule" or the "Parable of the Fireplace," but it is a provable and workable law that you (1) must give before you can get and (2) will get in direct proportion to what you give.

Luck is nothing more than opportunity. And, as you've seen, opportunities can be made. So, it follows that luck—which we constantly search for and complain about the lack of—can also be made.

DEFINE YOUR WEALTH VENTURE

You've been doing a lot of conscious thinking about your financial goals. It's time to define your goals, your general opportunity, then let the Mastermind System and the Power of Profit Motivation take over to give you the wealth you are searching for.

Take out a piece of paper. Let the Power of Profit Motivation work within you by doing these things:

- Write down your wealth goal.
- Put down a date for reaching your goal.
- Write down the short-range goals that will help you reach your major goals.
- Put completion dates on your short-range goals.
- Write down the general type of opportunity you have decided on using toward these goals.

Fold this slip of paper and put it in your pocket, wallet or purse. Take it out at least a couple of times a day and reread it. Think about your wealth goals every morning when you wake up and in the evening before you go to bed. Use the Power of Profit Motivation meditation steps from Chapter 1 as often as you can. If you come up with an idea—no matter how trivial—that will help you reach your goals, write it down on the back of your slip of paper.

Put something in—time and thought—and you will get something out—wealth and prosperity.

HOW TO MASTERMIND YOUR WEALTH VENTURE

Mike R. knew what he wanted and knew what direction it was in, but he wasn't sure of just how he was going to get there.

Mike had always wanted to own and operate his own trucking business. He knew that good percentage truck operators earned well over $50,000 a year from their home-on-wheels. When Mike set his financial goal and decided on his general wealth venture, he was working in the shipping out his basic long- and short-term goals so that he would start driving the company's own delivery truck within six months, get his semi-truck driver's license within a year, earn a promotion to the company's over-the-road trucks within a year and a half and drive for them at least two more years before buying his own line-haul tractor and going into business for himself. Mike also had a plan formulated to save money over the next three-and-a-half years so he could afford to buy his own equipment when the opportunity arrived.

Mike had built the framework of his future. His next step was to fill in the missing pieces and develop his opportunity into riches. He took the first step by starting a notebook on how to operate a successful owner-operator trucking business. He talked to truckers who came into the shipping department where he worked. He read magazines published for line-haul truckers. He sent for literature on trucks, equipment and business opportunities for owner-operators. He read, he studied and he planned. He learned what type of trucking operations are most profitable, how much expenses he should expect, how much to charge for hauling general commodities to make the highest profit, how to get good loads in major cities and how to buy and sell equipment. Mike thoroughly researched his wealth venture.

Then Mike started to take action. He made sure his superiors knew of his ambition to work into a driving position. He talked with their regular drivers to anticipate a transfer or an employee leaving. His first goal was to get into a driving job at his company. With goals and ambition, Mike made it with two months to spare.

Since then, Mike has taken and passed his truck driver's license test. He put in just over two years as a line-haul driver for his company, canvassing the nation. Today, he drives a new Peterbilt conventional up and down the West Coast for CenCal Electronics of Sacramento, California, and last year, he cheerfully paid taxes on an income of $63,000.

The Mastermind System of building your wealth venture into a high-profit enterprise is:

- Research your venture for profitability.
- Develop your venture into wealth.

MASTERMIND STEP #1

The Mastermind System is a systematic investigation of your chosen opportunity in search of facts, theories and applications that can be turned into profit. So, the first step to developing your wealth venture is to research your idea for the best method of serving others. Mastermind Step #1 is to *research your chosen wealth venture* by:

- Listing all possible and profitable methods.
- Ruling out more risky and less profitable ideas.
- Developing the best methods into your own wealth venture.

List All Methods of Developing Your Wealth Venture

For every type of business venture conceived by the Profit-Motivated mind of man, there are thousands of ways it can be developed into highly profitable wealth ventures. Its development reflects the skills, abilities and interests of the person who is building the venture.

Your Profitability Notebook (Chapter 4) is a great place to start listing all of the ways you can turn your chosen wealth venture into the highly profitable business venture you expect will carry you to your financial goal. Take a little time each day to go over your goals and basic wealth venture in your mind. Think about all the different ways it can be developed and write them down. None are too trivial or farfetched to be written in your Profitability Notebook. Remember, you are not passing judgement on which idea is best or how profitable it might be. You are just trying to come up with as many ways of turning your idea into riches as you can.

As an example, you could have chosen "buying and selling antiques" as your general wealth venture. Let's list as many possible ways to turn a profit in this field as we can:

- Specialize in buying and selling parlor furniture.
- Sell paintings from 1850 to 1925.
- Buy and sell brass lamps and spittoons.
- Deal in antique car parts.

- Sell old advertising trays, glasses and posters.
- Deal in antiques of the Old West.
- Buy and sell roll-top desks.
- Specialize in antique radios and phonographs.
- Sell old bottles.
- Find and sell old photographs and post cards.
- Buy and sell antiques of one geographic area or state.
- Salvage and sell antique fixtures from local historic buildings.

You get the picture. For every type of general wealth venture there are dozens of ways of *specializing* your way to profit.

Kelly M. deals in antique radios. He started at the age of 15, when he found an old radio in the attic of his home. His parents gave it to him to keep him occupied. Kelly began tinkering with the old radio until one day, to everyone's amazement, it began to work. Kelly was thrilled. He took it to a local antique dealer to find out if it was worth anything. The dealer offered him $50 in cash and threw in another radio that was not working. Kelly took it.

Kelly began asking around the neighborhood and soon found four more radios which he purchased for a total of $35. The remaining $15 went for a book on vintage radio collecting and repair, plus a few old tubes he needed. The five old radios netted him three newly varnished and working antique radios within a few months, and he found a market for them in a couple of days—the local radio station. They were glad to pay $175 for the three working radios which they put on display in their front lobby.

Kelly's inventory grew, and today, at 26, he runs a small shop in his garage that buys, repairs, refinishes and sells antique radios. His income is as large as many corporate executives', even though he started his unique business with no money. Kelly is on his way to wealth because he knows that specialization is where the profit is.

Eliminate Less Profitable Ventures

The next part of Mastermind Step #1 is to rule out the more difficult and less profitable methods of making money, which is a more subjective process. You'll have to decide which of the enterprises you've listed sound most enjoyable and profitable to you—and which do not. In the previous example of buying and selling antiques, you may decide not to deal with larger antiques because of space, cost or health reasons. You would then eliminate parlor furniture, car parts, roll-top desks, Old West antiques and, possibly, antique fixtures from your list of wealth ventures. Or, you may want to start with less capital and rule out ventures that require a large initial cost. You could then scratch parlor furniture, roll-top desks and, possibly, antique radios and antique car parts.

You should also rule out ventures that you have little interest in. Your chances of making a healthy profit are much higher with ventures you enjoy. In this case, you might decide not to sell paintings, lamps, spittoons or old bottles. You are narrowing the possibilities of your wealth venture to the *best* ventures.

Finally, you should rule out some of your proposed wealth ventures because they are less profitable than others. After studying the remaining options, you can see that buying and selling antiques from your area is too specialized or that there are already too many local antique dealers in your area.

By the process of elimination, based on our example, there are two wealth ventures in the antiques field that are most likely to succeed—and they could be combined into one—buying and selling old photographs, souvenir postcards, advertising trays, glasses and posters. We have eliminated those areas of specialization that require high starting capital, a large storage area, hold little interest and are less profitable. This example of how to eliminate less profitable wealth ventures can be applied to your own venture to bring you thousands of dollars in enjoyable profits.

Build Your Wealth Venture into Profits

The next part of the Mastermind System is to develop the best road toward your chosen wealth venture. There are three things you can do:

- Find a reliable source for your goods.
- Build a good clientele.
- Learn to price your goods or services for both high profit and quick resale.

These steps can be applied to any product or service-related business. Continuing with the example of an antique dealer who specializes in old photographs and related items, the first step is to find a reliable source or sources where these items can be easily purchased or traded.

Don C. decided to specialize in stereopticans, the slide viewers and cards that were popular before television arrived. After checking around, he found that the Midwest was the best place to find stereopticans and cards at reasonable prices. They were available at below collector's prices in small town antique stores, general stores and estate sales. Don even found a few good buys from large antique dealers who purchased them with large lots of antiques but weren't interested in smaller items. With letters and phone calls to the Midwest, Don found three good sources for the stereopticans.

Don lived near Los Angeles. He put an ad in one of the metropolitan papers: "**Stereopticans and Cards.** Unique and collectable. Hundreds to choose from. 5XX-XXXX." This ad drew dozens of calls each week. Don also sold his stereopticans on consignment at better antique shops in Los

Angeles. And, with the trade he got at area antique shows, Don quit his regular job within a year and now devotes full time to his profitable hobby.

The third part of developing the best method of marketing your wealth venture is to learn to price your goods for a high profit and quick resale.

Who sets the prices of merchandise in this capitalistic system? *The buyer.* In most cases, no matter where the seller sets his price he is only guessing at what the buyer is willing to pay. If he guesses right, he has a sale. If he guesses wrong, he doesn't. He then has to adjust the price to an amount he feels the buyer will be interested in.

The sale must also be profitable. If a seller offers an item for $5 which costs $5, he's not only not making a profit, he's also *losing* money on his own time and talents. So, the seller must price his merchandise or service based on *both* the cost to him and the value to others.

Don, the steroptician dealer, used the "Rule of Four" to price his merchandise. It means that an item purchased for $5 wholesale should sell for $20 retail. Or, reversed, he should pay no more than $5 for a $20 retail item. Don had little difficulty in finding sources for $5 stereopticans or finding metropolitan antique buyers who were willing to pay $20. Using the "Rule of Four," Don estimated that one-quarter of the eventual retail price went toward the wholesale price, one-quarter went for expenses of shipping and advertising, and one-half was profit for his labor and knowledge. Don realized that any of his customers could, if they desired, do the research and invest the time and money that he had, and purchase his merchandise at the wholesale price he did. Instead, they preferred to let him take care of the work and worry, and paid him more. They were happy, and Don was happy.

No matter what wealth venture you decide to start, one of the most important rules of success is to price your product or service to allow you a healthy profit while insuring a quick sale. This requires research of the value and price of your offering, plus motivation of others to pay what you are asking. It's all part of Mastermind Step #1: Research your wealth venture.

MASTERMIND STEP #2

Mastermind Step #1 has shown you how to find profit in your wealth venture. You've looked at many profitable ideas, you've ruled out the least likely to succeed and you've seen how to develop the best ones into a profitable wealth-building venture.

Mastermind Step #2 will show you how to develop that opportunity into a business that can offer you the income and security you've set as your goal. You'll learn how to start your business, find and keep customers and build your enterprise into an efficient money-making machine that needs less and less time, while offering you more and more profits.

So take out your Profitability Notebook and start taking notes. Your wealth venture, which can offer you an income of over $50,000 a year at home, is about to unfold.

START YOUR BUSINESS TODAY

The time to start is now. You know what wealth venture you want to build. You have set a financial goal. You are sure of where you would like to work. The next step is to put your business idea into action. All you have to do is:

- Set up your home office.
- Gather needed equipment and supplies.
- Set up your sources.
- Contact your potential customers.

Set Up Your Home Office

The benefits of having your business office in your own home are numerous:

- No wasted travel time to work.
- Personal tax benefits.
- Ability to buy a larger home.
- Savings on meals over restaurants.
- Closeness to family.
- Hire employees from family.

You can do everything at your home office that you can do at a downtown office—and more: You can take your lunch and breaks with your family; you can work late; you can quit early; you can take a day off without asking anyone; you can be your own boss.

To set up your own home office, you'll need space. For your first office, you can start with enough room for a desk and whatever equipment or supplies your business needs. It can be an extra bedroom, a corner of your master bedroom, your garage, an upstairs room or a travel trailer in the yard. As your business profits and grows, you'll want to plan your next home with at least one room—or maybe a whole floor—to include your business office.

Your home office must offer privacy. It must give you a spot where you can be alone to work out solutions to questions in your wealth adventure. You must be able to concentrate. If you work evenings, be sure a television is not nearby. If you are a housewife, plan to make your business hours coincide with the time when the children are at school or taking naps. You need a quiet undisturbed atmosphere in order to create and work.

Plan your first office right now: Where is it going to be? How much space do you need? How long can you plan to have your office there and still grow? Where could you have it if your business expanded faster? Could you enclose part of your garage? Do you have a camper or trailer that could be used as a temporary home office during expansion? Start setting up your home office today, and your wealth venture will soon be a reality.

Get Equipment and Supplies

Every business needs some type of equipment and supplies. Even the smallest service business will need a typewriter, a desk and stationery. If your wealth venture involves manufacturing or repair, you'll need even more. To develop a list of necessary equipment and supplies, answer these questions:

- What basic equipment do I need for my venture?
    —Hand tools?
    —Power tools?
    —Tables and jigs?
    —Storage bins?
    —Testing equipment?
- What power sources will I need? 110 volt? 220 volt? Other?
- Will I want to correspond with my customers and suppliers?
- What kind of recordkeeping system will I want?
- What is the minimum amount of equipment and supplies I will need to start my wealth venture?
- Are there any sources of equipment and supplies that offer substantial discounts to businesses?

Start to collect the basic equipment and supplies now that you will need to operate your business from your home. You may want to rent or borrow a typewriter rather than buy one until your business has grown. Or, there could be tools or test gear that can be rented to conserve capital. To start your business you need to ask:

- What equipment and supplies will I need?
- How much do I need?
- How can I get it with the least amount of capital?

Develop Your Sources

Whatever business venture you decide on will need sources of supply. If you manufacture or resell merchandise, you will need suppliers of the raw materials. If you sell a service, you are selling information and you will need to find sources of that information. Ask yourself:

- What is my major product or service?
- Where can I find sources for this product or service at a price that allows the healthiest profit while insuring quality to my customers?

Elmer J. makes windmills. His office is an old dinette table in the corner of his garage. His factory is a nearby workbench. Elmer has four sizes of windmills that he makes and sells as lawn ornaments. As he set up his business, Elmer started by using the local building materials company as his main source of supply. He got a builders' discount which allowed him to earn an eight dollar profit on each unit.

As business grew, Elmer started looking for a better source for the wood, paint and hardware that went into his finished product. He found a wholesale materials firm in a nearby industrial park that could better his profit by nearly two dollars a unit. Elmer saved an additional 50 cents a unit by picking up his materials, rather than having them delivered. While the quality was the same, the profit per unit increased by nearly a third when Elmer found a new source for his raw materials.

If your wealth venture is service oriented, you can still save money by finding more profitable sources of knowledge and information. If you are a mail-order book publisher you can search for a printer who charges less while maintaining the quality you need. If you are offering a consulting service there may be an association or group that can offer you a source of information that can be priceless.

Donna T. started an import-export business. After about six months of importing a dozen types of products for stateside customers she found an association of small importers that offered monthly publications, books and consulting services for dues of $75 a year. She gambled on a membership and sent in her check. Donna never regretted it. To date, Donna says she can attribute most of her six-fold growth in business to her membership in that association and the sources it has given her.

Contact Your Potential Customers

Your home office is ready, your equipment is in place and you've lined up your sources of supply. Now you're ready for your first customer.

How can you tell potential customers about your new business or service and motivate them to buy from you? Many ways. First, answer these questions:

- Who are your customers?
- What do you want to tell them about your business?
- How can you reach them at the least cost?

The first question is the most important one, because understanding your customer—and understanding how to motivate him to buy from you—is one of the keys to high-profit business. Who are your customers: Young? Old? Banker? Housewife? Cab driver? Business tycoon? Stereo buff? Coin collector? Who? What makes them buy? Are they also Profit-Motivated people? Are they looking for: Bargains? Quality? Service? Entertainment? Use a page in your Profitability Notebook to describe your average potential customer.

Why will they buy from you? What do you want to tell them about your new business? Do you offer the lowest price? Is your product unique and unavailable anywhere else? Do you deliver? Is your product or service guaranteed? Will this commodity save them money, give them security or make their life more enjoyable? What do you want to tell your customer in order to motivate him to buy from you?

The third question is: How can you motivate the most potential customers at the lowest possible cost? The best kind of advertising in the world is "word of mouth." But it's also the slowest. Quality workmanship and efficiency will speak for themselves in spreading the word about your wealth venture. To expand your market you need to advertise in a media that will reach the highest number of your potential customers.

If your customers are housewives, place literature on bulletin boards in laundromats and supermarkets. Advertise on the woman's page of local newspapers.

If your customers are antique collectors, tell them about your wares in a classified ad column offering antiques. Place a sign in front of your home. Pass your cards out at local antique shows.

If your customers are collectors, advertise in magazines and publications expressly for those collectors. Attend local shows. Visit local collector club meetings. Make yourself known.

Don't try to advertise to the general public unless *everyone* is a potential customer. If your customers are housewives, businessmen, landscapers, stamp collectors, or from any other specialized group, your most efficient promotion will be to that specific group.

Find out who your customer is, how to motivate him or her to buy, and go after him.

BUILD YOUR BUSINESS FOR TOMORROW

Your wealth venture is not an overnight get-rich-quick scheme. It's an opportunity for you to use the Powers of Profit Motivation and Leverage, combined with the Mastermind System, to build a highly profitable venture from a tested idea and little or no capital. You've been shown how to research and develop your wealth venture. Here, now, are the principles you'll need to understand to build your venture into an even larger enterprise.

TAKE YOUR VENTURE TO MARKET

For a couple of thousand years, marketing a product meant packing everything up before dawn and taking it to the local market place. You would rent a booth or lay a blanket on the ground on which to spread your wares in the hope that someone would come and buy from you.

In the name of progress man has vastly improved the marketing of goods and services, making him more efficient. Large companies market their wares by selling to wholesalers or distributors across the nation who take their profit and sell the goods to retailers who, in turn, take their profit and sell the goods to the ultimate consumer. Efficiency produces volume and volume lowers the cost of each unit so that, in many cases, the consumer could not duplicate the product for the price he is asked to pay.

The three major steps to profitably marketing your product or service are:

1. Analyze your potential customers.
2. Find out how to motivate him to buy.
3. Motivate him to buy.

Efficient Distribution Means Profit

Distribution is simply getting what you have to the people most likely to buy it. Each commodity offered has unique distribution needs. As you develop your own wealth venture, analyze your distribution problem with these methods in mind:

- Direct distribution by
  —Mail.
  —Freight.
  —Store or office or roadside stand.
  —Telephone.
- Indirect distribution through distributors.

The type of product or service you are offering will dictate or at least narrow down the methods you can use to distribute it. Antique furniture can't be distributed by mail or phone, but it can be distributed by freight, distributors or a storefront shop.

Take a look at your own wealth venture and decide which of the distribution methods are most efficient for you If there is more than one, decide on which is the most profitable. Efficient distribution of your product can add to the profits you expect to earn with your Profit-Motivated enterprise.

Promote Yourself to Wealth

To promote your product or service is to present it to the buying public in a way that will encourage them to buy from you with confidence.

Alva C. knew how to promote. Her chosen wealth venture was piemaking. Alva began by purchasing a used commercial oven and placing it in the attached garage adjoining her kitchen. She made two dozen pies, placed them carefully in her station wagon and took them to local restaurants. Alva offered them to the restaurant owners free of charge to encourage business. While she talked about the pies and cut a piece for the manager, she was also busy taking orders for the next day's pies. Within three weeks, Alva had as much business as she could handle.

But, Alva was an ambitious person. She bought a second commercial oven, put her two teen-aged daughters to work after school and early mornings and began promoting her *expanded* line of pies. At first, she gave each restaurant an extra pie every week if they would include "Pies by Alva, 5XX-XXXX" on each menu. It worked. The pies promoted themselves and Alva was forced to purchase a local bakery shop and move her operation out of her home by the demand for her promoted pies. Alva's two-year old business offers her a salary of $42,000 a year—and all the pie she can eat.

It's easy to promote something you believe in. Don't be afraid to tell as many people as possible about your new wealth venture and why they should buy from you. Invite your local newspaper over for an interview and sample of your commodity. Tell people in your clubs, church and neighborhood about your venture. Ask friends to tell other friends. Leave your business card anywhere you can. Advertise toward your specific customers. Tell on yourself.

It's not enough to have a good product or service. People must know about it. Promote yourself to riches.

THE MASTERMIND SYSTEM CAN BRING YOU WEALTH

The Mastermind System of building your wealth venture into a profitable enterprise means:

- Researching your venture for profitability.
- Developing your venture into wealth.

The Mastermind System shows you how to choose the most profitable method of exploiting your opportunities, then how to develop that venture by starting your own home office and marketing, distributing and promoting your product or service for the highest profits.

Follow these steps and you can Mastermind your way to riches.

THINGS YOU CAN DO NOW

The time to act is *now*. You have seen how to develop your wealth venture into a highly profitable and efficient business that you can begin at home. Don't stop—do these things *right now*:

1. Define your wealth venture. What kind of business have you decided will bring you the riches you're looking for?

2. Review the Mastermind System. Reread this chapter, making notes on how you can apply the methods offered to your own enterprise.

3. Mastermind Step #1: Research. List all of the possible and profitable methods of developing your wealth venture. Then, rule out the ones that are less likely to take you to your goals. Use your Profitability Notebook to develop the best of these ventures.

4. Mastermind Step #2: Develop. Start your business today by setting up your home office, gathering the equipment and supplies you need, setting up your sources and contacting potential customers. Then, develop the best method of marketing, distributing and promoting your venture.

5. Decide. Plan your profit goals for next month, quarter, year and five years. Take your wealth venture off paper and put it into action.

6 Think Profit Motivation.

7

Build Your

"GOLD"

Reserves

You've discovered **GOLD**.

You've learned how to set your own goals, organize your search, locate the right opportunity and develop that opportunity into riches. These are the mileposts on your road to riches.

The next four chapters will show you how to develop the **GOLD** Formula into the wealth and success you are searching for. They will fill the gaps between the mileposts to give you a clear and easy-to-follow map of your individual road to success.

This chapter will show you how to reach your own personal goals by setting short-range goals — and how to use my Fail-Safe System to *insure* success.

FILL THE GAP BETWEEN WHERE YOU ARE
AND WHERE YOU WANT TO BE

Lloyd G. knew where he wanted to go. He wanted to own property worth over $1,000,000 and live off the rents it earned. That was his goal. After looking around, Lloyd decided the best way to reach his goal was to:

- Get the highest paying job he could.
- Invest at least 50 percent of his earnings in high-risk ventures.

Lloyd then broke his sub-goals into even shorter range goals: look for the right job for one month, spend three months preparing for the job if necessary, plan to spend three years on the job, search for the right high-risk opportunity, use leverage to purchase the property. Lloyd saw the wide gap between the $645 he had in the bank and his goal of $1,000,000 in property, so he broke his goal into shorter range goals and took them one at a time.

Lloyd had heard that certified welders were in high demand on construction projects in Alaska and that they could get as much double-overtime as they wanted. Lloyd checked it out. The rumor was right. One company Lloyd wrote to offered him a job in a town in southern Alaska that allowed almost year-round work and a wage nearly eight times his current wage. By brushing up on his welding skills and trading his car for a well-insulated camper, Lloyd was ready and on his way to wealth.

Lloyd found that he could work up to 14 hours a day without straining his health, and he kept his expenses down by living in his camper. When he arrived, he discovered that a shortage of fresh beef created a perfect market for a short-range investment because construction workers were willing to pay almost any price for it. He contacted a friend in the Northwest who had a few head of cattle and had one butchered and flown up. It was sold within three days at a profit of *1200 percent*, and the workers were asking for more.

In three years, through working, investing and saving, Lloyd was worth over $400,000. He was nearly half way to his goal. Lloyd kept his job for another two years. and with land investments in Alaska and Washington, Lloyd is now over two-thirds of the way to his $1,000,000 goal and expects to retire with a sizable income at the age of 38. Lloyd reached his seemingly impossible goal by setting shorter range goals that took him where he wanted to go.

PICK YOUR OWN FATE

Your long-term financial goal is like a port you want to reach. You know what and where it is, but you haven't charted your course. You could just start your engines and hope you make it — or you could plan your voyage, anticipate and prepare for expected rough seas and navigate yourself to wealth. The decision is yours.

Take out the piece of paper you carry with you that has your wealth goal on it. Study it. How far away from that goal are you right now? When do you reasonably expect to reach your goal? By what date? What logical steps are there between where you are and where you want to be? Write them down, too, because they are the stepping stones to your goal.

HOW TO PLAN YOUR FORTUNE

How realistic is your goal? Now is the best time to analyze it before you finally decide to develop it to its fullest capability with the powers you have. The Goal Success Formula says that *any* goal can be reached if:

- You are willing to do the things necessary to reach it
- Your goal is more valuable than the things you must do to reach it
- Your goal is within the realm of human accomplishment

Decide now whether your own personal goal is worthwhile, valuable and attainable. If, after analyzing it, you feel that it isn't, modify it or throw it away and find one that is worth your efforts. Be sure that the goal you set is the one you want, because *if you develop your goal with the Power of Profit Motivation you are assured of success.* If you follow the **GOLD** Formula and use the rules of success in this book *you cannot fail!*

USE THE POWER OF PM TO REACH YOUR GOAL

As you remember, the Power of Profit Motivation is the power of the conscious and subconscious minds to clarify and act on well-defined problems and goals because they have been motivated to do so with a positive end result.

The steps to harnessing the Power of Profit Motivation are:

- Define your problem or goal clearly.
- Motivate yourself toward that goal.
- List methods of reaching your goal.
- Outline your short range goals.
- Meditate on the problem.
- Be prepared for the solution.

In the first half of this book, you read dozens of success stories where people of average intelligence and ability have harnessed the powers of their mind and built their own future as they wanted it with the Power of Profit Motivation. You can, too.

The Power of Profit Motivation can be unlocked with the powers and principles of meditation and auto-suggestion.

You've set your goals and found a method of reaching them. Profit Motivation will help you with the many decisions and moves you must make to reach that goal. Unlock the Power within you to build your road to riches with these steps:

- Find a completely quiet place to relax. Sit back in a comfortable chair and let your daily problems vanish for a few moments. Don't worry about anything. Turn out the lights and become aware of your mind. Completely turn off your physical senses.
- Remind yourself of how valuable your goal is to you. See yourself enjoying that goal. Picture yourself touring many $100,000 homes until you find the one you want. See yourself driving the car you've always wanted. Watch yourself give your loved ones the things they've always wanted in life.
- Tell yourself, "I have the Power within me to earn riches and find happiness in such great abundance that I can easily share both with others." Repeat it. Keep this sentence on a small card with you in your pocket or purse. Remind yourself that you have the Power to make it come true.

The Power is there. The Power of Profit Motivation can bring you the things you believe you can have. Grab hold of the Power *now* and let it take you to where you want to go.

Clarence and Kay had a dream of owning their own small-town weekly newspaper. But they were just dreams — until the day they discovered the Power of Profit Motivation. They began to plan their dreams into action and within six months they found a run-down newspaper for sale at a distress price. Using the Power of Profit Motivation and the principles of capital leverage, Clarence and Kay purchased the business with just $1,000 of their own cash.

They then used the principles of Wealth Development, outlined in the second half of this book, to build the newspaper's income nearly 60 percent the first year. They sold out later with a profit of over 1,000 percent by using the Power of Profit Motivation in their daily business.

Review Your Wealth Worksheet

It's time to review the Wealth Worksheet you filled out with Chapter 3. You've since seen the entire **GOLD** Formula untold. As the road to success has been outlined for you, you may have modified your goal or clarified how you expect to get there, so take out your Wealth Worksheet and see how it can be improved.

- Have you thought of any other expenses in your current budget?
- What additional luxuries would you now add to your desires for tomorrow?
- Is your final financial goal the same now as it was when you filled out your Wealth Worksheet? If not, revise it.
- How about your deadline for reaching your wealth goal? Should it be changed?
- Are you willing to invest more time and money in your future now that you see how it can pay you back many-fold?
- Are your steps to your wealth goal still the best? Is there a shorter way to your goal? Can you add a few more short-range goals?
- Sign and date your Wealth Worksheet again.

This exercise of reviewing and revising your Wealth Worksheet will help you clarify your goals and help you analyze the best way to reach them. As you grow in the principles of success outlined in this book, you will want to periodically revise your Wealth Worksheet.

Review Your Skills Worksheet

Look over your Skills Worksheet in the same way. Do you now see other skills you have that could be made profitable? How? Revise your Skills Worksheet as you increase your knowledge and ability.

How to Step Toward Your Future

There is a wide gap between where you are today and where you want to be tomorrow. In fact, the distance may seem insurmountable. It may look like you can never reach your financial goal. And you can't — unless you take it a step at a time.

Step-by-Step Goal Simplification shows you how to break your major goal into smaller, easier-to-reach goals that will take you to where you want to be. Step-by-Step Goal Simplification will show you how to make your time more profitable, how to find success today, and how to set yearly, monthly, weekly and daily goals that will carry you to your plan of earning over $50,000 a year at home.

How to Make Your Time More Profitable

There are two ways you can make your time more valuable:

- Increase your hourly worth.
- Increase your productive hours.

Every minute of your 1440-minute day is worth money — and the more skillful and enterprising you become, the more your time is worth. If an hour of your time is now worth $5 and you have set your goal at earning over $50,000 a year, all you have to do is increase your hourly worth to $25. Reaching a goal of earning $25 an hour for a 40 hour week sounds more attainable than earning $50,000 a year, doesn't it? It's a matter of taking big goals and breaking them down into small, easy-to-digest goals that you *believe* you can reach.

The second way of increasing your worth is to find more hours in the day. Impossible? Not at all. Nearly everyone who has not sat down and managed his time can find one to five hours each day that can be put to profitable use. They are hidden in many places:

- Early morning hours (this book is being written between 6 and 8 am by a non-early bird)
- Lunch hour (time to read motivation and business opportunity books and use your creative thinking powers)

- TV time (face it, television is more of a habit than a pleasure. Cut down or eliminate your TV viewing and you will add many profitable hours to your future)
- Weekends (weekends are for family activity and one of the finest things you can do with part of your weekend is use time to build their financial future with a profitable enterprise)
- Vacations (many new enterprises have been started during vacations from regular jobs. Is there a day or a few days that you can borrow from your next vacation to help you set up your own enterprise?)

Just how much is your time worth? That's a decision you have to make. If you feel you are worth $5 an hour, then finding more hours in the day offers only a small profit. But, if your time is actually worth $25 an hour or more — and I'm sure you know it is — then remember your true worth when you sit down in front of the television for a couple of hours. Your profitable enterprise may not pay you what you are worth right now, but it will eventually. Believe me, if you follow the success formula outlined in this book, your time will be worth much more than just $25 an hour.

How to Set Yearly Goals

You've set your wealth goal. To illustrate the road to your success, let's say that your goal is earning over $50,000 a year at home within three years. You can modify the rules and illustrations to fit your own — possibly greater — goal.

Your goal, again, is to earn an income of over $50,000 a year from an enterprise that can be operated from your own home or any other place you choose, and your deadline for your goal is set at three years from today. That's a huge jump from where you are to where you want to be if you don't keep in mind:

Ramsey's Law: One goal at a time, one step at a time equals SUCCESS.

You've got 3,744 hours available each year when you are not sleeping or working. How much of this surplus time are you willing to invest in your future? And, between now and your three-year deadline you have a total of 8,237 hours in which to find and build your wealth venture. I'm not going to suggest that you use them all to build your fortune, but you can see that there are thousands of hours available to you that you can turn into money by planning your time better. By investing some of these hours into an honest search for a more profitable tomorrow, you'll find it.

Howard F.'s goal was the same as yours, $50,000 a year within three years with a business operated from his home. He quickly figured that if he doubled his income for three years it would reach just over $50,000 a year. That was his plan. So, all he had to work on his first year was increasing his income from $7,000 a year to $12,500. Howard didn't even try to worry about earning over $50,000 because he knew that — at this stage of the game — $50,000 was almost beyond his imagination. So, he sat down to plan how he could nearly double his income in a year to reach $12,500.

Howard decided to start by investing 728 hours his first year (or 14 hours a week) to doubling his income. Quick division of his time into the amount of additional earnings he needed told Howard that all he had to do was earn $7.50 or $8.00 an hour during these spare hours and he could reach his first year's goal.

Howard chose a mail-order bookstore as his wealth venture and he was on his road to riches.

How to Set Monthly Goals

Howard's final wealth goal of $50,000 a year was broken into smaller, easier-to-reach goals: $12,500 a year, $25,000 a year, then $50,000 a year. Howard was now breaking down his first major goal — to earn over $12,500 in the coming year — into smaller monthly goals. To reach his goal he needed $5500 a year more than he was earning now. That's about $460 a month of extra income after expenses, and Howard had planned about 60 hours a month in which to earn it.

Howard had decided to specialize with his mail-order bookstore and only sell numismatic books to coin collectors. As suggested, he searched for his most profitable customers and considered how to reach them. He found that the best method was to advertise in the classified section of the major coin collector publications. He ordered 200 letterheads and envelopes, used the first 50 to write for information on ad costs and book suppliers, then sketched out the business he would need to reach his monthly goal.

Estimating book costs at 60 percent of retail, mailing and advertising costs at another 20 percent, Howard estimated his gross should be about $2300 a month to reach his first year's goal. With an average retail of $10 a book, Howard figured that he had to sell about 230 books a month with approximately $2 profit per book.

Howard was taking a large, seemingly unmovable amount of money — $50,000 a year — and breaking it down into smaller and more manageable mounds, then shovelfuls, until he discovered short-range goals that he could easily handle. Every shovelful was bringing him closer to his $50,000 goal.

How to Set Weekly Goals

Howard now had a much more manageable goal: sell about 230 books a month at about $10 each. He broke that goal down again to be 56 books a week. He also realized that if he sold a $20 book, it was as good as selling two $10 books as far as his goal was concerned. So Howard decided to use the lower priced and more popular numismatic books in his ads to draw collectors in, then use his mailing list efficiently to interest them in higher-priced books.

By shopping around, Howard found a supplier who was not only closer to him than most of them, but who also offered to help him with his advertising costs and drop-ship some books that he had less call for.

Howard wrote to the numismatic publication's editor explaining his new business venture and was pleased to read a story about it in just a few weeks. This "free advertising" brought Howard inquiries for over $1500 worth of books during the first month.

Howard began listing other ways he could increase his income:

- Offer 10 percent discounts to clubs for books bought in quantity (Howard saves on advertising costs).
- Start a coin collectors book club with monthly selections at reduced prices (and reduced wholesale costs).
- Use numismatic mailing lists to encourage collectors to update their knowledge with books about their hobby.
- Increase his buying power for larger wholesale discounts.

How to Set Daily Goals

Howard was on his way. By breaking his larger goal into smaller goals he was finding the success he wanted.

Howard set his daily work schedule like this:

- Monday thru Friday — two hours each evening.
  - —Pick up orders at the post office
  - —Sort and record orders.
  - —Fill orders.
  - —Package orders.
  - —Mail.
  - —Correspondence, ordering and inventory.
- Saturday morning — four hours.
  - —Special project.
  - —Promotion.

Howard set aside part of an extra bedroom for his business, the Numismatic Book Store. In it, he had a desk, work table, books, supplies, postage equipment and files. He easily operated his business from his home office and more than reached his goal of $5500 in profits from his part-time enterprise. Combined with his regular job, Howard earned over $12,500 his first year.

Looking back over his goals, Howard told me recently that the next two years of doubling his income were actually *easier* than his first year in business. He reached every one of the goals he set for himself — most of them ahead of schedule — and now devotes full time to his lucrative enterprise that offers him an income of over $50,000 a year from his new home.

Howard reached his goal one step at a time — and so can you.

Sketch out your own plan for reaching your financial goal. Answer these questions:

- What is your goal?
- How soon do you wish to reach it?
- Is it realistic?
- What steps do you need to take to reach it?
- What timetable can you put on these steps? Set your goals by time: monthly, weekly, daily.
- What is the first step you must take toward your wealth goal?

YOUR FAIL-SAFE SYSTEM FOR WEALTH

Thousands of otherwise intelligent, creative and ambitious people are stopped from enjoying the riches they are entitled to by *fear* — fear of failing. They are afraid that they will never succeed, so they never try. Potential millionaires are now sitting at someone else's office desk. Knowledgeable inventors and creators are making things — and high profits — for someone else. Skills, knowledge and creativity are being wasted because of the fear of failure.

Don't let the fear of failing stop you from reaching out and grabbing what you want from life. It's yours. All you have to do is build your own unique Fail-Safe System for wealth. The Fail-Safe System is like an insurance policy against failure—though it costs you *nothing*. It can take the risk out of your wealth venture. It can offer you the freedom and security you need to start your business with confidence. It can make the difference between success and failure.

As newspaper readers learned during the cold war of the 1960's, a fail-safe system is a method of insuring safety should a system fail to operate properly. And a fail-safe point is a predetermined point which a system can reach and still turn back from without loss.

Your wealth venture Fail-Safe System can insure against loss and failure with:

- Outside income.
- Alternate profit sources.
- Alternate methods.
- Bail-out system.
- Fail-Safe point.

Your Fail-Safe Insurance Policy

Wouldn't it be great to find an insurance policy that would insure you success in your chosen wealth venture? You can write your own policy — at little or no cost — by building your own Fail-Safe System into your business enterprise.

The first thing your Fail-Safe Insurance Policy should cover is income. You need income to live. You don't want your wealth venture to drain or dry up your current income. You want it to add to what you're making today. Two ways you can insure against loss with your new venture are:

- Additional income from your regular job.
- Getting contracts and reliable customers.

There are many ways to earn additional income from your present job to help insure that your wealth venture will not take funds from your regular income. You can offer to work overtime and holidays, you can earn and ask for a raise, you can step up into a job with more responsibility and more income, or, if you're paid by what you produce, you can increase your productivity. Often, a few dollars of extra income a week will keep your wealth venture from taking funds from your regular income and help build your success insurance policy.

If you are already engaged in your wealth venture, look toward getting more dependable sources of income such as contracts, or developing customers you can depend on to buy regularly from you. Their business will be like money in the bank for your young venture and drown the chances of failure.

Alternate profit sources can also be found so that if your enterprise doesn't work as well as predicted, you can easily switch your attention to another source and continue building your business and profits.

If your venture involves selling products, look now for related products that can also be sold. Howard, the coin book dealer mentioned earlier, eventually branched out into selling books on other hobbies. He knew from the start that if he couldn't make enough profit from coin books, he had alternate profit sources by selling related products. This knowledge helped him put confidence in his business as well as dollars in his pocket.

The same can be done with businesses that sell services. A business consulting service should also consider offering lectures to business groups and publishing booklets on business topics. The idea is to find alternate sources of profit to insure a healthy wealth venture.

Your Fail-Safe Insurance Policy will also cover finding *alternate* methods of developing your primary venture. If your venture is a vending machine route, you can look at the alternative method of setting up an arcade of vending machines at one location rather than one or two machines at many locations. This can easily be applied to amusement vending machines such as pinball machines and video games. If your business is a consulting service, an alternative method to contacts by walk-in and letters would be a phone consultation by appointment. Customers would call you at an appointed time to discuss problems with you by phone, whereby you will both save time.

You can also insure against failure by carefully looking at your wealth enterprise for more efficient methods, doing the same old thing in a different way. What modifications can you make to your venture that would make it a more unique and valuable product or service and thus help insure your success?

How to Bail Out

There are no 100 percent failure-proof businesses. But there are ventures that are 100 percent loss-free. You will be more confident of your success if your Fail-Safe Insurance Policy offers a provision for eliminating all financial losses. And, you can write your own policy if you do these two things:

- Buy at resale value or below. Make sure that everything you buy such as equipment, supplies, and raw materials, is purchased at the lowest price available so that it can be easily resold without loss or returned to the supplier for full credit.
- Find alternate customers. Every business field has liquidators who will buy new merchandise near cost and resell it to the general public at below retail. Find out who can do this in your field of venture and learn what price they will pay for equipment and supplies before you purchase them.

You can eliminate losses by buying at the lowest price possible and finding alternate customers for your merchandise and equipment. It's part of your Fail-Safe Insurance Policy.

How to Find Your Wealth Venture's Fail-Safe
Point

To fully insure yourself for success, you must make sure you have done everything you can do *before* you invest much time and money. You must find your wealth venture's Fail-Safe Point and do everything you can to insure success before you reach it. To find your venture's Fail-Safe Point, ask these questions:

- How many units or dollars must my venture produce to be profitable?
- How much time and money can I afford to invest to insure my success?
- How much planning and preparation do I need before I start?
- How can I recapture any losses if necessary?
- What can this wealth venture offer me?
- What's stopping me?

By planning your wealth venture step-by-step, finding its Fail-Safe Point and writing your own Fail-Safe Success Insurance Policy, you can insure yourself against failure and earn thousands of dollars of honest enjoyable profit in the years to come.

THINGS YOU CAN DO NOW

Write your own *Success Insurance Policy.* Follow the principles of this chapter and do these things *right now:*

1. Use your Power of Profit Motivation to study your wealth goal. Meditate on your main goal and see the natural steps leading to its fulfillment.

2. Set your short-range goals. Break your main goal into yearly goals, monthly goals, weekly goals and daily goals. List the steps you need to take toward your goals — then take them.

3. Look at your first short-range goal. What can you do today — right now — to complete that goal? Do it.

4. Build your own Fail-Safe System. Write your own Fail-Safe Insurance Policy by searching for income sources, alternate methods, knowing how to bail out and setting your own Fail-Safe Point.

5. Think Profit Motivation.

8

How to

Create

Money

You are an entrepreneur. You organize and manage business enterprises by increasing initiative and decreasing risk. You found companies. You invent products and create services for profit. You are always looking for the "quick dollar"—and often find it. You are Profit Motivated.

So far in this book, you've learned how to take your first step toward your fortune at home through a small enterprise that requires little or no capital, while offering the golden carrot of high profit. Now it's time to take the profits from your first venture and multiply them in either a related or completely separate enterprise. You are going to organize your search for even higher profits.

HOW SAM C. CONTINUED TO BUILD HIS FORTUNE

Sam C. built his first fortune with an investment of $300 and an idea for a weekly classified ad publication (see Chapter 4). Within a few years, his investment grew to over $1 million, but Sam wasn't satisfied. He wasn't a publisher; he was an entrepreneur, a business builder.

Sam had always been interested in electronics. He had some schooling in basic electronics but didn't understand the new and complex solid state theories. However, he knew someone who did. Sam also knew that the key to future profits for thousands of enterprising people would be through electronics, and he wanted to cash in on the opportunities available. Sam took a gamble—he rented a small building near his publishing firm, equipped it with electronic gear, hired Frank, his electronic genius-friend, and turned him loose to "invent something."

After more than seven months of 12-hour-a-day work and dozens of false starts, Frank hit upon something. He found a way of filtering liquids with sound waves. He could suspend and trap foreign particles with a machine that gave off different sound frequencies. Frank saw a handful of uses for his invention, but Sam saw *hundreds* of possibilities: cleaning huge pots in food processing plants, purifying blood in hospitals, even filtering beer in the brewing process. Frank was the inventor, and Sam was the entrepreneur. Frank was offered the security of a regular wage and a comfortable place to work, while Sam took the initiative and risks and—with the Power of Profit Motivation—reaped the financial rewards.

You can find your second fortune by using the income and knowledge you earned in your first fortune to search for greater wealth in the spreading world of profitable enterprises around you.

HOW TO ORGANIZE YOUR SEARCH FOR MORE PROFIT

The steps to your second fortune are the same as those to your first: Set your goals, organize your search, locate the right opportunity, and then develop it with Profit Motivation.

The first step to organizing your search for greater wealth is to design your profitability goals. What kind of and how much profit are you looking for in your next enterprise?

Decide right now to operate your businesses primarily for profit. If you enjoy what you're doing, all the better. But, an entrepreneur must make decisions about profit based *only* on the rules of profit and not on the rules of emotion. If profit tells you to expand your business with well-trained experts and emotion tells you to hire your friends and train them to the task, your success will be found by following the rules of profit.

Rule One of Profitability: As much as possible, leave your emotions out of profit decisions.

The next step in designing your profitability goals is to see how they correspond with your Wealth Worksheet goals. Test each idea for profitability against your long-range financial goals and see if that opportunity can help you bridge the gap between where you are and where you want to be. Will your new enterprise help you reach your short-range goals on time? Can you develop this new enterprise with a minimum of capital? What risks are involved? How can you minimize them? What can you do to insure success?

Sam C.'s profitability goal was to earn his second million within three years. For that opportunity, he was willing to gamble five percent of his potential return, or $50,000, for initial capital. He minimized his risk, then he took a calculated gamble and won. He set his profitability goal, he made decisions based on facts rather than emotion, and he used the Power of Profit Motivation to take him to his goal.

Find a Need, Then Fill it

Your second fortune venture will, in many ways, be like your first. One important link is that both will be based on finding a need that a large group of people have, then searching for a way to fill it in exchange for some of their money. How can you find this unfilled need? Ask yourself:

- What do people need?
- What do people want?
- What needs can I fill?
- How can I fill these needs?
- Is it profitable for me to fill these needs?

A *need* is a lack of something wanted or thought necessary. People need shelter, food, clothing, love and self-esteem. More specifically, people need a comfortable shelter that offers adequate room to sleep, eat and entertain. To elaborate on that, people need a kitchen with a stove that offers easy usage and uniform cooking. Even more specifically . . . well, you get the picture. You can break *basic* needs into *specific* needs.

As needs become more refined, they are accompanied by wants. A *want* is something desired but not fully necessary. A *want* could be a self-cleaning oven or a microwave oven. Even so, the wants of some are the needs of others. Your job as an entrepreneur is to find needs and wants and decide if and how you can offer solutions to others for a profit.

What needs can you fill? What are your skills? What special knowledge or interests do you have? Are you mechanically inclined? You could earn top profits by buying and installing major appliances for builders and remodelers. Are you more interested in using than fixing appliances?

Start a microwave cooking school and combine it with microwave oven sales to your students. You have hundreds of potential business enterprises within you when you search for a need and look for a way of filling it for profit.

How can you fill these needs? In our example, you could purchase or rent a small van that travels from site to site installing appliances or giving cooking classes to neighborhood groups and selling ovens. Finding a source of supply for things necessary for your second wealth venture is easier than it was the first time, because you now have contacts and experience in buying and selling that can be worth thousands of dollars in profits.

To fill a need for profit, ask yourself what you would do, as an enterprising person, if you had this need to fill for yourself?

The last question is the most important: Is it profitable? Can you earn your second fortune with this venture? What is the risk involved? Is the risk worth the investment necessary? Rough out on paper how much you can charge for your product or service or how much time and materials are necessary and how much each is worth. Show whether there is a clear profit that can be increased with skillful management by an experienced entrepreneur.

Where to Look for Profit

The major idea I'm trying to offer throughout this book is that potential for profit is all around you—everywhere you look. It's just a matter of learning how to see the world with a Profit-Motivated eye and think things through with a Profit-Motivated mind. You'll find highly profitable business ventures waiting for you to discover them in nearly any direction you look, whether it involves home, business or recreation.

Your home is your castle, and even though the drawbridge creaks and the moat needs cleaning, you work hard for the money you need to buy and maintain it. Your regular job and your profitable enterprise offer you money so that you can give yourself and your family the enjoyment of a fine home. Your customers are exactly the same; They have both needs and wants for their homes. By searching your own castle with a Profit-Motivated eye and mind, you can find many ideas for ventures that will fill both your customers' needs and your own. Here are a few profitable opportunity idea starters:

- Is there a need for quality storm windows in your area?
- With increased interest in fireplaces, would a chimney sweep or firewood supply business be profitable?
- Would a burglar alarm or security patrol business be profitable?
- Could you offer a home emergency service that offers plumbing, electrical and heating repair service at any hour?
- How about a housecleaning service for shut-ins, rental owners and builders?
- Could you offer a home landscaping and tree-trimming service?
- Would a remodeling service be profitable in your area?

The list of profitable ideas around the home is endless. Walk through your home with a notebook in hand and see your home as an entrepreneur. You'll soon have a long list of profitable ventures from which to choose the best and the easiest.

The business world offers hundreds of other potential second fortune builders. They could be small enterprises with one employee, which could be operated as a subsidiary to your main enterprise, or they could be full-scale business ventures. Here are a few examples:

- Can you paint signs and stencil holiday greetings on storefront windows?
- Do you have a profitable knowledge of labor relations you could offer to businessmen for a fee?

- Can you offer a combination office service for the one-person office: typing, dictation, mimeographing, letter writing, mailing and bookkeeping?
- Can you do market surveys for local businesses?
- Can you organize local business people into a group and become its executive secretary?
- Can you counsel others on how to start and build a profitable business?

The third field to review for profitable enterprises is one that has built more quick fortunes than any other—recreation. As people gain more money and surplus time, the recreation industry grows—and the potential for high profits grows with it. Here are a few ways you can profit from this growth in recreation:

- Offer lessons in your favorite sport: skiing, baseball, pool, bowling, hunting, skating, swimming, race car driving, fishing and so on.
- Buy and sell used camping and sports equipment.
- Offer guided excursions into nearby wilderness areas.
- Publish a newsletter for local or regional enthusiasts in a popular form of recreation.
- Purchase a recreational enterprise such as a bowling alley, sports shop, skating rink, amusement hall or slot track.
- Rent recreation equipment to others.
- Operate a gymnasium or health farm.

Whatever recreational enterprise you choose, you can be sure that profits will be high and quick if you get in early. Recreational fads are the riskiest—and the most highly profitable. Plan your recreation enterprise as you would any other, with market research and product knowledge.

Higher profits from your wealth venture can be found not only in new enterprises but also in making your present wealth venture more efficient. You can reach your own wealth goal more quickly and easily by learning how to develop more profitable methods.

How to Develop New and More Profitable Methods

Wealth is everywhere—from the creation of new ideas to the improvement of old ones. By using the Power of Profit Motivation and the secrets of success outlined in this book, you can bring fresh profitable ideas to nearly any phase of business. Added wealth can be found by applying the Power of PM to:

- Opportunity concept.
- Opportunity development.
- Opportunity application.
- Opportunity promotion.
- Opportunity sales.
- Opportunity distribution.

Whether your opportunity is a product or a service, you can creatively build profit in each part of the business cycle. The opportunity concept is the first germ of an idea that comes to you. By setting aside time to use your Power of Profit Motivation, you can come up with dozens of potentially profitable ideas in just an hour or so. And, after you've chosen the most profitable opportunity, you can use the Power of Profit Motivation to apply your service or manufacture your product, promote it, sell it and distribute it. It can all be done with the Power of Profit Motivation.

In both Chapters 1 and 7, you saw the steps to tapping the Power of Profit Motivation used to help you reach your personal wealth goal. The same concept can be used to reach any goal or solve any problem. Apply the Power of Profit Motivation to your everyday life by following these steps:

- Find a quiet area in your home or office where you will not be distracted or bothered. Shut out the world. Close your eyes and picture the most calm and relaxing scene you can: A crystal clear lake in late spring, the ocean at wintertime, a concert hall. Leave all of your problems and frustrations out of your mind for awhile. Completely relax.

- Slowly and deliberately describe your problem to an imaginary person. It could be a real person such as a kindly uncle, father, mother or best friend. Or it could be someone invented by your imagination. Talk about your problem or situation. Ask questions. Answer questions. Don't feel pressed by time or urgency.
- List in your mind the possible solutions to this problem. What are the alternatives? What is the best way to solve the problem or find a better solution? Ask yourself what you would advise your imaginary counselor to do if he or she brought you this problem. Keep your wealth goal clearly in mind as you probe your subconscious for the answer. Use the Power of Profit Motivation to find the solution to any problems you encounter on your way to your wealth goal.

These steps will open your mind to the Power of PM and help you find better ways of increasing your productivity and creativity. These steps can be applied to any of the six parts of business opportunities: Concept, development, application, promotion, sales and distribution. Use them and you will find new and better ways of developing more profitable methods of operating your wealth venture.

How Lloyd L. Used the Power of Profit Motivation to Solve Problems and Find Success

Lloyd L. had a problem. He operated a janitorial service in an area where competition was high. He needed to develop a new and more profitable method of offering his service to others so that he could stay ahead of the competition. He decided to search for the solution with the Power of PM.

Lloyd went to bed early one evening and rose early the next morning so that he could have the house to himself for a couple of hours. He went into the front room, put a Hawaiian music record on the stereo, climbed into his favorite chair with a cup of coffee and relaxed—with the lights off. Lloyd told himself he would take care of the day's problems later and shut them out from his mind. Then he pictured himself sitting on a beach in Hawaii. The sun was warm, the huge waves orchestrated a relaxing sound and washed all his problems away. Lloyd was completely relaxed.

Next, Lloyd brought an old friend into his dream, a friend whose concern and knowledge Lloyd respected. They both sat on the beach, talking about anything that came to mind. After awhile, Lloyd asked his friend what he would do with a janitorial business to make it innovative and profitable. The friend seemed to think for a moment, then took a stick out and wrote in the sand: E-X-T-R-A M-I-L-E. Then the friend explained, "Lloyd, I'd try to let my current customers do all my advertising for me by going the extra mile with them. I'd spend a little more time waxing and buffing that floor, so that both management and employees would be impressed by its brilliance and cleanliness when they came in the next day. I would spend just a little more time to make things sparkle. I would leave pens and matchbooks on desks with my firm name on them. I would put special work into cleaning spots from high-traffic areas. In other words, Lloyd, I would not only go the extra mile, but I would do it in a way that would have my customers talking well about my service to others."

Lloyd had the right idea. He turned on the light, took out a pad and pencil and began writing down ideas. "Change firm name to '*Sparkle* Janitorial Service'." "Plan an extra 15 to 30 minutes at the end of each job for leaving a lasting impression on the customer." "Leave business cards on the front desk of customers' businesses." "Go that *extra mile*."

Lloyd is no longer in the janitorial service business. He's now head of EM enterprises, a firm that franchises Sparkle Janitorial Service throughout the Midwest. His salary is over $100,000 a year, and Lloyd has plenty of spare time to spend it—because he used the Power of PM to solve a problem.

You can use the Power of Profit Motivation to develop new and more profitable methods of building your current wealth venture by:

- Clearing your mind.
- Looking at the complete problem.
- Listing the possible solutions.
- Deciding on the best solution.

It's the Power of PM!

How to Diversify Profit Sources for Greater Wealth

Now that your first wealth venture is a success and you are nearing your first financial goal, it's time to look for ways to build and keep the wealth you've earned. You must diversify your profit sources.

Why should you diversify? Why should you have a variety of profitable enterprises? To give you:

- More income

  with

- Less risk.

An entrepreneur or business-builder can just as easily make his or her fortune by operating an amusement arcade as he can by owning a car wash. The rules of success that are learned in one type of business can be applied to nearly any other. If, as an entrepreneur, you can build a $100 investment into a $10,000 profit, why not take $1,000 and build it into $100,000 in another enterprise? By diversifying your enterprises, you can increase your income 10-, 20- or even 100-fold, and diversifying can also lower the risk by spreading it among many enterprises. If you own a car battery manufacturing firm and a competing entrepreneur invents a 10-year battery, your business could fall off drastically, and you may be forced to close down. But, if you own four or five diverse business enterprises, and the same thing happens, you can afford to drop the least profitable and continue making your fortune with the rest.

There are two directions you can head in when you decide to diversify your wealth ventures:

- Spin-offs and related ventures.
- Separate developments.

Spin-offs are the easiest, because they are just a modification of the enterprise you have now. If you have a car battery firm, you can spin off by selling tires, battery cables and car accessories. A taxi service can diversify its profits by delivering packages for local businesses or even leasing cars. For every wealth venture, there are at least half a dozen spin-offs and related ventures that can bring you added wealth with minimal risk.

To find natural spin-offs to your first wealth-building enterprise, ask yourself:

- What natural spin-offs come to mind?
- How are similar businesses diversifying?
- What new spin-offs could be used?
- Which spin-offs and related ventures would be most profitable?
- Which spin-offs would be the least risky?
- What spin-offs and related ventures could I start with little or no additional capital?

To truly diversify your wealth venture, you should also look at separate developments or opportunities that can offer profits unrelated to your first wealth venture. They will minimize your risk by spreading profits over the entire business cycle. Here's how to find separate opportunities:

- Review your list of possible wealth ventures, which you made earlier in this book.

- Study financial publications for methods of investing surplus profits.
- Talk to other entrepreneurs about their own wealth ventures.
- List additional ideas as they strike you, and spend time researching each idea for profitability.
- Read other Parker Publishing books on profitable enterprises.

Let's carry our example of a car battery manufacturer further and say that he has made a good income by selling batteries wholesale and retail. He is now interested in completely diversifying his profit sources in case the car battery market drops off. He might consider a list of second wealth ventures like this:

- Trophy manufacturing.
- Pro bowling shop.
- Radio-TV repair and sales.
- Quick-print shop.
- Used bookstore.
- Correspondence school.
- Business consulting service.

You can diversify your profits by using the facts you've learned about profit-making in completely different fields. Discover what you've learned from you first wealth venture by writing down basic knowledge you've learned about!

- Customers.
- Products and services.
- Distribution.
- Administration.

The principles of business that you've learned in your first wealth venture can be applied to dozens of other businesses by asking yourself:

- What makes customers buy a product or service?
- What kind of product or service are they most interested in buying?
- What is the best way to sell and distribute a new product or service?
- How can I administrate my business most efficiently?

CREATE MONEY FOR PROFIT

There are two sources for ready cash to help you build your second fortune:

- Your first wealth venture.
- Financiers you've met.

The best way to pyramid profits is to use profits from your first venture to build your second and succeeding wealth ventures. As your original venture begins to grow, set aside a percentage of "surplus" profits to help you begin your next venture, and you will soon find that you have enough money to start your new enterprise and build it to its highest potential.

The other way of finding diversification funds is to contact financiers that you've met or heard about as you built your first venture: bankers, private parties, investors, friends. If your first venture has a good track record of earning profits and paying bills, you can be assured that financiers will be more than willing to help you with the capital you need for expansion or diversification.

You can also combine the two methods for quick funds. Begin your second venture with the leverage of your own funds *plus* funds borrowed from others. You are minimizing risk and maximizing profits by using the principles of leverage and other people's money.

Fast Money Techniques

Leverage: the advantage or power gained by using a lever to move a large object with the amplified power of a smaller object.

The physics of leverage are easily applied to the world of profits. Physics tells us that we can move something with a fulcrum and a lever that is otherwise too heavy to lift. The fulcrum is placed near the object to be moved and the lever is laid across the top of the fulcrum and under the end of the object. The strength of the person on the other end of the lever is magnified many times—depending on where the fulcrum is placed—and he can move objects that he could not move otherwise.

You can apply this simple rule of leverage to your own enterprise. You can use a small amount of money to gain something worth a great deal more money with the leverage of rented money. That's right, you can rent money with leverage.

Don P. wanted to purchase a new piece of equipment for his home-operated machine shop. The equipment was priced at $12,000. Don knew that he could earn at least $12,000 in profits in the first year he operated the machine— if he could buy it. Don decided to use the Power of Leverage to purchase it.

Don talked with his banker and convinced him to rent (or loan) him $10,000 to purchase the machine. Don came up with the remaining $2,000 and the machine was soon his. In the first year, Don did earn over $12,000 in profits with his new machine. How much did he make by using leverage?

Don rented the money from the bank at 10% interest and made a total of 600% on his original $2,000 investment.

The "golden rule" of money: If you can find the opportunity to rent money at one rate and make it earn a higher rate of interest, do it!

Where to Rent Capital

There are many places where the smart entrepreneur can go to rent money. One of the most important is public financial institutions such as banks, savings and loans, finance companies and mortgage bankers.

Banks and finance companies are the best sources of smaller, short-term loans with personal property or just your signature as collateral.

Savings and loans institutions and mortgage bankers loan money using real property as collateral for longer terms.

Other credit sources for renting capital are:

- Private financiers.
- Trade credit.
- Factoring.

Private financiers are people who would much rather earn 10, 12 or 15 percent or more on their money than put it in the bank where they earn only half as much. As you develop your wealth enterprise, you'll meet many of these private financiers who are willing to loan you capital for a worthwhile venture. In fact, as your capital grows, you may consider becoming a private source of capital for other entrepreneurs.

You can also use other people's money to make profits by taking advantage of *trade credit*. If your supplier offers you a large amount of merchandise with 90 days in which to pay for it, he is actually loaning you the money for 90 days. If you can sell the merchandise at a 200% profit during the 90 days without paying interest to your supplier, you have made a full 200% profit on other people's money. You have used the power of trade credit. Check with suppliers to see which ones offer the best trade credit terms and do most of your business with them.

Another way of renting money for profit is to *factor* or borrow money against your accounts receivable (list of people who owe you money). There are many factoring firms who specialize in different types of businesses. They either loan against accounts receivables or purchase them outright at a discounted price. In either case, you are getting cash today for promises to pay tomorrow. A smart entrepreneur can easily turn today's cash into two or more times what tomorrow's money will be worth. Ask your banker about factoring.

How to Prepare Your Venture for Financing

When you take your second wealth venture idea—or any other financial need—to your financier, you'll need to show him how you expect to repay the loan. He wants to know in black and white how you plan to use the funds. He will want to see three things:

1. A pro-facto financial statement
2. A current financial statement
3. Your performance record

A *pro-facto financial statement* is a fancy term for a statement that shows what you plan to use the money for and how it will be profitable enough to repay the loan. It will outline what capital is needed, what it will be used to purchase and how the purchased items will earn a profit. Document your facts and you're on your way to a smooth loan.

Your *current financial statement*, showing how much your current enterprise is earning and how much you are worth, will also be needed to display your net worth and credit rating.

The bank or financier will also be interested in your *performance record.* They'll want to know something about the field in which you make your profit, what expertise or special knowledge you have, and something about other successful enterprises you've had. A simple letter, outlining your experience and background, is usually enough.

Package these three statements together, and you can present them to financiers listed in this chapter and in Chapter 2. You'll be on your way to renting other people's money and turning it into high profits with your own second wealth venture. You'll be creating money. You'll be an entrepreneur.

THINGS YOU CAN DO NOW

You're learning how to create money. Keep up the momentum. Here is a list of things you can do *right now* to grow your own money tree:

1. Decide to be an entrepreneur. Be a creator of profits. Buy and sell enterprises for the profits involved rather than on emotional values. Be Profit Motivated.

2. Develop more profitable methods. Start looking today for better ways of building your first wealth venture to increase profits and decrease risk.

3. Diversify your wealth venture. Open your eyes right now to additional wealth ventures. Use the principles of spin-offs, related ventures and separate developments to earn even higher profits.

4. Use fast-money techniques outlined in this chapter. Use the power of leverage to move mountains. Talk to financiers about how you can rent money to build even higher profits. Document your ideas.

5. Think Profit Motivation.

9

Dynamics Method
of
Increasing Profits

The average entrepreneur earns high profits; the smart entrepreneur has *others* making high profits for him.

You have the power within you *right now* to motivate others to bring you higher profits than you could earn yourself. You can persuade others to work harder for you or buy more from you. You can show them how they can help themselves by helping you. You can motivate them to do things for you that they wouldn't think of doing for anyone else. You have the power to motivate others with your own *Dynamics*.

HOW JEANETTE F. TAUGHT OTHERS TO MAKE PROFITS FOR HER

Jeanette F. built her first fortune with a small stuffed animal business. She began with a sewing machine in an extra bedroom and—using the Power of Profit Motivation—built her business within a year to five employees working from her converted garage. Jeanette was working 14 hours a day, six days a week and earning $35,000 a year.

One day, Jeanette got smarter and decided to double her income with half as many hours. Using the principles of Dynamics that you'll soon read about, Jeanette planned the road to her new goal.

The first thing Jeanette did was to gather her "factory" together for a meeting. She told them that she wanted to turn most of the responsibility of her business over to her employees and, in turn, let them earn more of the profits. She asked them to vote on working by-the-piece rather than by-the-hour. They were unanimously in favor of working by-the-piece.

Then she showed them how much it cost to make and sell each of their products and asked them to bid on how much they would charge to make the necessary parts on a piece-meal basis.

Finally, she brought out her incorporation papers which showed that Animals N Stuff, Inc. was now a stock company with ownership divided among those who owned stock. Jeanette gave each employee one stock certificate for each month they had worked for her. The employees, now part of the management, were elated.

In the following months, Animals N Stuff, Inc. nearly doubled its business: Productivity rose, profits rose and Jeanette's salary rose, while her hours dropped. The employees only owned 20 percent of the stock in the new corporation, but you would think they owned all of it, by the way they worked for the good of their firm. Jeanette used

Dynamics and Profit Motivation to turn a small garage business into what is now a million-dollar-a-year enterprise with 14 employees.

It's the Power of Dynamics.

HOW DYNAMICS CAN BRING YOU WEALTH

You can motivate others to bring you higher profits by showing enthusiastic interest in their personal needs and goals—and then showing them that they can fill those needs by doing something for you. You are motivating them with your enthusiasm.

The Power of Dynamics can easily be applied to everything you do to bring you wealth, success and happiness. You can build your own personal enthusiasm for what you are doing by following these three easy steps:

1. Review your accomplishments.
2. Reflect on them.
3. Recognize them.

You can build your Self-Dynamics by searching your own life for accomplishments within it. Have you reached one or more of your wealth goals? Have you started your own wealth venture? Is your wealth venture offering a needed product or service to others? Will your wealth venture offer jobs to others? Will your wealth offer opportunities to others?

It's hard to be subjective, to reflect on ourselves. Most of us are tougher on ourselves and our accomplishments than we are on others. See yourself as someone else would; trade places in your mind with your best friend. For a few moments, he has your job, your life, your goals—and you have his. How's he (you) doing? How would you rate his (your) success in life? What could he (you) do to improve it? Study your own life as your best friend would and you'll build your own Self-Dynamics.

Finally, you must recognize your accomplishments for what they are—success. Have you made positive steps toward your wealth goal? Are you working toward more? Are your goals honest and realistic? Are you interested in reaching your goal? Do you have the power to reach it?

Take an honest look at yourself and at your accomplishments and plans, and you will build your own Self-Dynamics and personal enthusiasm for what you are doing.

HOW TO USE DYNAMICS

Dynamics can be used on others to make them feel more important and to help you toward your own wealth goals.

The Power of Dynamics can be used:

- On customers.
- On suppliers.
- On employees.
- On other important people.

You can motivate customers to buy from you with your enthusiasm by showing them how they will benefit from what you have to offer them.

You can motivate suppliers by enthusiastically showing them how they will profit from their growing sales to you.

You can motivate employees by enthusiastically showing them how they can earn more money and make their job more enjoyable by working harder for you.

You can motivate other important people—such as officials, financiers, stockholders and celebrities—by showing them, with enthusiasm, how they can benefit by giving you favors and working with you.

You can motivate others by recognizing your own accomplishments and by using enthusiasm to show others how they can reach their own goals by working with you.

How to Develop Selling Dynamics

There are two types of selling—internal selling and external selling—and both can be improved with Selling Dynamics.

To accomplish any worthwhile goal you must first sell yourself. This is called internal selling. Then you must sell it to others for profit. This is known as external selling. Success means selling yourself and selling others.

To sell yourself with Selling Dynamics you must:

- See.
- Study.
- Savvy.

Frank T. wanted to motivate himself to sell vacuum cleaners. The first thing he did was to take a good look at his product. He studied the models he planned to sell and looked at competitive models. He took a machine apart and examined how they were put together.

Then Frank studied them by taking a course in vacuum cleaner repair. He studied the differences and similarities between the vacuums he had explored. He studied them to find out why women purchased new vacuums.

Finally, Frank recognized the most important points of vacuum cleaner sales—he had savvy. He recognized what the customer was looking for. He recognized the features and benefits of each of his products and how to point them out to his customers.

Frank sold himself first.

To sell others with Selling Dynamics you need to

- Show.
- Sketch.
- Sell.

After Frank T. had motivated and sold himself on the value and benefits of his vacuums, he had to convince his customers that what he believed in was true for them also.

First he would show them his line of vacuums, from the smallest to the largest model, showing them how they could find one in his line that would fit their cleaning needs as well as their pocketbooks.

Then Frank would narrow down the choice to two vacuums that he felt would probably best fit their needs and would begin sketching their features and benefits. He drew a verbal picture of the customer using the machine. He mentioned how easily they operated. He described the extra attachments and how the customer would use them in everyday cleaning. He sketched the quality of workmanship that insured the customer of carefree ownership.

Finally, Frank sold his customers by letting them operate the machines while he described the benefits of owning a new and modern vacuum. He sold them on the low cost per month versus the high value of his vacuums and let the vacuums sell themselves.

These are the easy steps to Selling Dynamics. Salesmanship is one of the highest paid professions in the world. You can earn higher profits for your own venture or build a brand new venture with the easy-to-apply principles of Selling Dynamics. To sell yourself: See, study, and savvy. To sell others: Show, sketch, and sell.

HOW TO MOTIVATE OTHERS FOR HIGHER PROFITS

Your success is going to be partially based on how well you motivate others to do what you wish them to do. You must motivate customers to buy from you. You must motivate suppliers to sell to you. You must motivate others to promote your business, help you build your business and offer supporting services.

You can easily motivate others to do what you wish them to do with the Power of Profit Motivation. You can motivate customers by saving them money or offering more value or service for their dollar. You can motivate your suppliers to give you their best prices by showing them how they can profit. You can motivate others to help build, promote and operate your business by finding their need and helping them fill it as they help you fill yours.

You can motivate everyone you come in contact with everyday to help you toward your goals if you help them toward their goals by:

- Recognizing their needs and goals.
- Enthusiastically showing them how they can reach them by helping you reach yours.

No matter who you talk to or what you talk about, you can motivate people to your way of thinking with the Power of Profit Motivation and the principles of Selling Dynamics.

To reach your goal, help others reach theirs.

This principle can be applied to all types of day-to-day contacts:

- In-person.
- Telephone.
- Mail.
- Advertising and promotion.

By combining the Powers of Profit Motivation and Selling Dynamics you come up with a powerful and easy-to-use formula for motivating others to do things you wish them to do:

- Get their attention.
- Hold their interest.
- Build their desire.
- Earn their action.

Let's see how this PM/SD formula can be applied to your wealth venture and daily life.

Get Their Attention

There's a $50 bill stuffed into page 214!

Now that I have your attention, I'll tell you how you can gain someone's attention by finding their primary need or interest and showing them how you can help them fill it.

Most of us are so wrapped up in our own needs and interests that we often forget others. We don't realize that the best way to fill our own needs is to fill the needs of others. You can come up with the best invention since electric light, but if no one *needs* it you'll never sell it.

Sometimes you even have to show people a need they really didn't know they had until it was pointed out. A good example of this is the deodorant and personal product ads that saturate radio, television and magazines. They build a need—then show you how you can fill the need with their product. To get your attention in the first place these ads dramatize a real or imagined need. They show you how you *need* their product to be socially acceptable and fresh all day. They sometimes go a step farther and brand you an outcast if you don't use their product. They have gotten your attention.

Others get your attention by showing you how you can earn more money, live a longer life, have sex appeal or youth, by using their product or service. They motivate you be getting your attention with statements like:

"Get in on the PROFITS in SMALL ENGINE SERVICE and repair."

"Make BIG MONEY at home with your own WHOLESALE BUSINESS."

"PRICES SLASHED. Closeout by Swiss watch importer."

"FREE. New electronics catalog."

"NEVER be LONELY again!"

You can do the same. You can use these principles to gain the attention of others who can help you with your wealth venture. Whether they are customers, suppliers or anyone else important to your venture, you can gain their attention by finding their greatest need or desire and showing them how you can fill it for them. Here are examples of attention-getting statements for common home business ventures:

Antiques—	"HUGE PROFITS from the past."
Correspondence school—	"MAKE $50 AN HOUR in your own saw shop."
Import-export—	"Enjoy gifts from AROUND THE WORLD."
Bookkeeping service—	"Never WORRY about TAXES again."
Mail-order bookstore—	"Let us bring the BEST SELLERS to you."

Hold Their Interest

Now that you have their attention, you must hold their interest by elaborating on your statement and showing them what they will have when their need is filled by you. As an example:

MAKE $50 AN HOUR
in your own saw shop.

Yes, you can earn $50 an hour and more with your own saw sharpening and sales business at home. You can work your own hours at your own pace and earn wages over ten times greater than the average American. All you need is a few basic tools and the easy-to-understand course offered on saw sharpening . . .

This type of interest-holding statement will work well in your own business literature or advertisement. For in-person or telephone contact you can try the positive question approach—asking questions that will be answered with a "yes".

> *"Mr. Johnson, would you like to earn*
> *$50 an hour?"*

> *"Would you be willing to invest just*
> *a few hours of your own time to*
> *learn a profitable skill?"*

> *"Would you pay $5 a week to learn*
> *this skill that can bring you*
> *as much as $2,000 a week?"*

To hold their interest, show them what they will have when they fill their need.

Build Their Desire

How can you turn their interest into action? By showing your customer, supplier or other contact that it is easier to fill his need through you than it is to go without.

With confidence and enthusiasm, you can build their desire with statements like:

> *"The few cents a day this service costs*
> *will save you many dollars."*

> *"You'll find life easier and more*
> *rewarding when you earn the*
> *higher wages of a professional*
> *auto mechanic."*

> *"A simple signature on this form will*
> *cure your money problems."*

"If you sell me these supplies at
this price you'll increase your
turnover and your profits."

Earn Their Action

Help them make a big decision by making a smaller decision that infers the big decision has been made in your favor.

"Would you prefer a blue sedan, or
would the red one be best
for you?"

"Put your 'okay' on this slip and
the set you want is yours."

"Do you want to take it home with
you or would you prefer we
delivered it this afternoon?"

Get your contracts' attention, hold their interest, build their desire, then earn their action and you've sold your ideas with Selling Dynamics and the Power of PM.

HOW TO TURN ADVERSITY INTO DOLLARS

No person or opportunity is perfect. No matter what business venture you decide on as your wealth venture, there will be obstacles to overcome, problems to solve and adversity to face. The average person will often face a major problem and give up. The entrepreneur will face the same problem and decide how it can be turned around into prosperity and profits.

Jean S. started a bookkeeping service operated from her home in a small Midwestern town. Three months after she started, a flood wiped out 31 homes—including hers.

Her home-office was gone, her records were gone and her wealth venture was gone.

But, Jean made up her mind not to let adversity knock her down, and she started looking for a way to rebuild. Her insurance agent relieved some of her worries by telling her that she was fully covered. Jean moved in with a nearby friend until her home could be rebuilt. Then, she began looking around for a way of rebuilding her business.

The idea came quickly. Soon after the flood, state disaster relief funds and all of the paperwork involved to apply were offered to the townspeople. Jean quickly printed up a letter for local flood victims, telling about her book-keeping service and special interest in the area and offering to help victims take care of the large amount of red tape involved to process their claims. Almost two-thirds of the victims responded, and she was soon busily at work, turning adversity into profits while helping her own neighbors. When tax time came around again, you can be sure whom the local residents called to work on their taxes.

Find the Silver Lining to Every Cloud

For every adversity, there is an opposite and equal prosperity. All you have to do is find the "silver lining" to the cloud. You can find the benefits to misfortune, calamity and distress by:

- Building the positive.
- Eliminating the negative.
- Knowing when to quit.

Accentuate the Positive

You can find the positive side of any adversity by making a list of the negative points to a situation, then making a corresponding list of positive points. Some of the positive points might sound ludicrous, but they will help you sort out your problem and help you find the best method of overcoming it.

Jean S., the bookkeeper who was flooded out, wrote a NEGATIVE/POSITIVE LIST that looked like this:

NEGATIVE	*POSITIVE*
Trauma of disaster	**Opportunity for reevaluation of life and values**
Home destroyed	**Can rebuild better home with insurance funds**
Damage to personal belongings	**Belongings can be replaced; memories remain**
Future business uncertain	**Opportunity to build new business and life from ground up**

You can do the same for any adversity that you must face in your business or personal life. Again, some of your positive statements may sound ridiculous, but state them anyway. They will help you see the "silver lining" in every cloud.

Eliminate the Negative

Your Negative/Positive List will also produce a number of negative parts to your problem that can be eliminated. Jean S. eliminated the negative point of uncertain future business by quickly finding another related wealth venture.

To eliminate the negative points to your own problem, ask yourself: What steps would I have to take to turn this problem into an advantage? Some problems are built on soft foundations, and by removing as many of the negative points as possible—putting them on the positive side—you can often solve the entire problem.

Building the positive and eliminating the negative points to a circumstance could also be called "looking for opportunities." As an entrepreneur, you are becoming an expert at finding opportunities, while others pass them by. By looking for the "silver lining," you can find even greater and more profitable enterprises in the rubble of adversity.

Know When to Quit

Chapter 7 showed you how to establish your Fail-Safe System for wealth, as well as how to bail out of a business venture before it costs you more than it is worth. Careful planning of your venture before you enter it can often help insure your success, but if you must drop an enterprise because of unprofitability, turn it into a profitable education by:

- Listing your mistakes.
- Outlining how you would do it over again.
- Consider the profitable education you've received from the opportunity.

By getting a profitable education from every opportunity you tackle—even the financially unprofitable ones—you can continue to build your worth on your way to an income of over $50,000 a year at home.

How to Learn from Your Mistakes

Everyone makes mistakes—but your profitable future depends on how much you can learn from these errors in judgment and how much of that education you can apply to future opportunities.

You can learn from your own mistakes by:

- Accepting your errors.
- Accepting yourself.

You can learn from the mistakes of others by:

- Finding out what they did wrong.
- Subjectively analyzing the error.
- Deciding on the best *positive* action.

Barbara L., who was opening a telephone answering service, talked with Mrs. B. about her telephone answering service in a neighboring town. Mrs. B. said that one of her biggest mistakes—one that cost her the most profits—was not keeping better records of customers' incoming calls. Barbara L. decided that the best way to improve this situation in her own proposed answering service was to develop a padded form that she could fill out as people called in. It would have spaces for all important questions and a reminder of what to ask the customers—depending on the type of business she was taking calls for. Barbara learned from the mistakes of others and saved herself thousands of dollars in profits by keeping her customers informed and loyal.

How to Rebuild

Operating a business from your home is a learning process. You try to anticipate problems and solve them before they cost you money. You try to find new ways of serving your customers and earning more profits for yourself. But, what if you have to back away from a wealth venture in order to save your investment? How can you rebuild your wealth venture?

First, you have to *clear the rubble*. That is, you have to salvage as much of your venture as you can. You have to sell some of the equipment or supplies you don't plan on using in your next venture and keep the rest for future use.

Next, you should *check the foundation* to make sure that your basic idea is solid and that you can rebuild on it without having further problems.

Then, you should *estimate the cost of rebuilding* to assure yourself that the profitability is worth the cost in time and dollars of rebuilding.

Finally, you should *move into action* and start construction of your new wealth venture on the cleared foundation of the old.

By rebuilding your new opportunity on the foundation of the old, you have better insured your success than if you started a completely new enterprise in an untried area. If your first wealth venture sours, decide on how much of it can be salvaged before going on to your next opportunity. With the Power of Profit Motivation, you can literally profit from every mistake.

GREATER SUCCESS WITH THE TWO-POCKET FORMULA

Business is gambling. You study the odds and make plans. You make a decision and you put your stakes down. How much you win or lose depends on how much you are willing to gamble and the risks involved. My *Two-Pocket Formula*—which you'll see in a minute—will show you how to take much of the risk out of gambling in business. But first:

Risk and the *risk factor* refer to the probability of future loss. That is, a high-risk business is one where there is a high chance of loss sometime in the future. As an entrepreneur, you realize that your goal is to maximize profits while minimizing risk in business. Developing a profitable balance between risk and returns is your major goal.

Why does one type of investment offer you 5-1/2 percent return on your invested money while others offer 9,

15, 100 percent and more? The returns differ because of the difference in the amount of risk that you may lose all or part of your investment. Of course, a wise entrepreneur can use the Power of Profit Motivation and other success formulas to increase profits while decreasing risks, but business in general offers a direct relationship between risk and return.

How can you anticipate and project the amount of risk involved in an opportunity? One way is to use *Ramsey's Opportunity Ratio*, offered in Chapter 5. You can also anticipate risk by making a list of the major things that could go wrong with your venture and analyzing the probability of each event occurring.

As you do, remember the rule of compound risk: the higher the number of risks, the higher the total risk. As an example, if the risk factor of your being able to buy supplies at a low enough price to resell profitably is 80 percent—and you feel the chances of finding enough customers to buy them at a profitable price is also 80 percent—your total risk factor is not 80 percent, but 80 percent times 80 percent or 64 percent. You are *compounding* risks. Of course, this book has shown you dozens of ways of decreasing this risk to a profitable level, but the rule of compound risks shows you how risks work together.

You can minimize risk in any part of your wealth venture by:

- Decreasing costs.
- Increasing sales.
- Choosing the best risk-to-yield opportunities.

If your product or service costs you less to offer than your competitor's, you can make a higher yield or profit on your investment and thereby decrease risk.

If you find a better way of increasing customers or sales, you will increase your yield for the amount of risk involved.

If you choose the best risk-to-yield opportunities, you will increase your chances of profits while decreasing the chances of less than success.

How to Reinvest Profits

As you follow the successful business concepts outlined in this book and your profits grow, you will want to reinvest some of your surplus profits into other wealth ventures. Some of them will be high-risk ventures and some will be low-risk opportunities, but the idea will be the same—get the highest yield for the lowest risk.

Your future investments of surplus profits will be based on two things:

- Financial availability.
- Financial needs.

First, you must decide on how much surplus money you have to reinvest. Does your wealth opportunity give you $100 a week, $1,000 a month, or a lump sum of $5,000 $20,000 or more to invest in future profits? As you find yourself with surplus profits, decide on just how much you can reinvest.

Then, decide on how much you expect that investment to yield. Do you need an investment that will give you a lump sum or an income of so many dollars a month for a certain period? Do you expect your $1,000 investment to yield $10,000? $3,000? $100 a month for 3 years?

The product of financial availability and financial needs is the *risk*. As you have seen, the return on your investment is in direct relationship to the risk you take. That is, if you expect to parlay $1,000 into $1,000,000 you should prepare yourself for the obvious high risk involved.

How to Gamble in Business and Win

As promised, my *Two-Pocket Formula* will show you how to take much of the risk out of business.

When Jack M. goes to Reno to play the slot machines he takes half of his gambling money and puts it in his right pocket—and places the other half in his left pocket. As he plays the slot machines or other gambling games he takes betting money from his right pocket only. When he wins, he splits his winnings in half and puts half back into his right pocket and half into his left pocket. Whether Jack's playing roulette, blackjack or the slots, he follows the same rule: set aside half your winnings.

If Jack's luck runs bad and his right—or playing money—pocket is empty he simply reaches over into his left pocket, counts out *half* of the total and fills his right pocket again. Jack can do this split many times before he—on an extremely unlucky day—loses everything.

What Jack is doing is diversifying his risks. Jack gambles with half and saves half. His right pocket is for high-risk ventures and his left pocket is for low-risk ventures.

That's the Two Pocket Formula: Diversify your risks by putting part of your surplus money into high-risk ventures and part into low-risk ventures.

As an example, if your wealth venture offers you a lump sum of surplus money totaling $10,000, you can diversify your risks by placing half (or any fraction) in a bank or municipal bonds, while the other half goes into higher risk ventures.

One investor I know has set a budget for his family that is quite liberal. Any surplus income over his household budget is split three ways:

- 40% goes into savings or similar low-risk investments
- 40% goes into high-risk business and land investments
- 20% goes into a travel and recreation fund

You can lower total risk and increase profits tremendously by using my Two-Pocket Formula—and the Power of Dynamics.

THINGS YOU CAN DO NOW

You are an entrepreneur. You can turn high-risk/low-yield ideas into low-risk/high-yield business ventures. You know the principles and the power of success. You are on your way to even higher profits as you do these things *right now:*

1. Use your Power of Dynamics. Build your own enthusiasm for your accomplishments and plans to motivate yourself and others.

2. Decide how you can motivate others for profit. What needs can you fill for others? How will you get their attention? Hold their interest? Build their desire? Earn their action?

3. Learn how to search out and profit from "silver linings." Use the principles and ideas in this chapter to turn adversity into profits. Learn from your own—as well as others'—mistakes.

4. Use the Two-Pocket Formula in developing a plan to invest your surplus profits. Minimize risk and increase yields for greater profits.

5. Think Profit Motivation.

10
Getting Your
Full Share
of Success

You're getting closer to reaching your wealth goal. You're on the verge of earning $50,000 a year at home with a wealth venture that is not only profitable, but enjoyable. You're learning how to build your own worth to over four times that of the average American. You're learning how to apply the versatile Power of Profit Motivation.

This chapter will offer you quick, easy and valuable steps that will take you to your final wealth goal—and beyond. This chapter will show you how to plan for success by priorities, how to make decisions and how to continue your successful goal-setting.

Keep reading—every page can be worth thousands of dollars to you.

HOW BEN D. STAYED ON THE TRACK

Ben D. now has a very profitable vending machine route in a large metropolitan area. Two years earlier, Ben had started his business with $500 and a lot of great plans. He was soon making a good wage for himself, but he was working 14 or more hours a day to earn it. Even so, Ben felt he wasn't getting the most important things done.

Then, a banker-friend gave him an idea in a few minutes that eventually made Ben thousands of dollars—and cut his working time almost in half. The banker showed him how to work by priorities. He reminded Ben that the conscientious businessman will always find a duty to fill his time: checking the books, trying to get just one more customer, developing more wholesale sources, cost-cutting and other jobs. The banker told Ben that the smart businessman takes things—not in the order of their appearance—but in the order of their importance to his own goals.

As an example, the banker asked Ben to take a pencil and paper and write down everything he had to do the next day. Ben's list had:

- Take daily deposit to bank.
- Order two new machines.
- Read trade journals.
- Service current accounts.
- Look for new business.
- Review accounts payable.
- Repair defective machines.
- Take truck in for regular servicing.
- Talk to Johnson about building maintenance.

Then the banker asked Ben to read over his list again and mark a "1" by the most important thing he had to do, "2" by the second most important thing and so on.

Finally, the wealth-wise banker told Ben to start the next day by reviewing his list, tackling job "1" until it was completed, then moving to "2" until it was done.

The next day, Ben followed the banker's suggestion and decided to complete as many high-priority jobs as he could before 5 P.M. Within two weeks, Ben found that his days were much shorter—and that he seemed to be getting more things done. At year's end, Ben's total income was up 43 percent, a result, in part, of his new ability to work by priorities.

HOW TO DEVELOP YOUR WEALTH VENTURE TO THE FULLEST

You can continue to build your own wealth venture above and beyond your own goal by using the Power of Profit Motivation to set and evaluate short-range goals. Here are six ways to higher profits through the Power of PM:

- Find more customers.
- Encourage repeat business.
- Ask for referrals.
- Reduce expenses without reducing quality.
- Use leverage even when you don't need to.
- Learn how to make big decisions.

When you go fishing, you don't put steak or pizza on the hook—you put worms. Why? Because fish don't really care what your favorite food is; they are only interested in their favorite food. The same idea can be applied to "fishing," for more customers. You'll never bring customers in by telling them how much money you hope to make off them. You'll only earn their business by telling them how they will benefit from buying from you.

So, to fish for customers, go to the most populated fishing hole and use their favorite bait In other words, decide on the best method of reaching the most potential customers, and show them how they can get something they want from you.

Successful wealth ventures are built on repeat business—selling the same customer over and over on replacement or related products or services. To encourage repeat business remember the three things that make people buy in the first place:

- Quality.
- Service.
- Price.

With some exceptions, the larger firms often dictate prices that smaller ventures cannot control or sometimes cannot even compete with. Service is labor related and, since at least half the cost involved in most businesses is labor, it is the area through which the smaller venture can earn the highest profits while encouraging repeat business. The small business—under $1 million in sales a year—can offer the customer service that very few larger firms can compete with.

The third method of increasing your wealth-venture income is to ask satisfied customers for referrals because of the quality of your product or service. One man who sells cars on weekends from a vacant lot gives an extra price reduction by handing out cards to customers saying he will give them $25 in cash if a friend of theirs brings the card back when they buy a car from him. Other businessmen make regular calls to satisfied customers every few months to keep their friendship, encourage repeat business and ask for referrals. If your customers have been truly satisfied with the quality of your work, this method can bring you thousands of dollars in new business every year.

Cost-cutting is one of the best ways of increasing your business profits—as long as your quality of product or service remains high. Here are three ways you can reduce expenses without reducing quality:

- Quantity buying.
- Shopping for sources.
- Eliminating the middle man.

By estimating and planning your needs for a needed item you can often buy in larger quantity for a greater discount. Another way of earning such a discount is to buy with other similar businesses through an association or informal trade group. Quantity buying of supplies and equipment can mean a savings of as much as 60 percent in costs.

Wholesale suppliers are much like retail stores in the spread of their prices. By shopping for wholesalers, as you would for groceries or a new car, you can often pick up an additional savings of 10 to 25 percent.

Depending on your buying power and needs, some businesses can buy direct from a factory and eliminate the middle man. Check with manufacturers for the size and price of the minimum order they will accept and save as much as 30 percent.

How to Use Leverage—Even When You Don't Need to

The principle of using leverage in buying for higher profits is not just for those with little capital. In fact, even the largest firms still use leverage to buy merchandise or property when they could pay cash for it. They realize that the percentage of return on their capital is higher as their leverage ratio moves higher.

Tom H. chose a taxi service for his wealth venture. He refinanced his home and received $10,000 in cash equity. He kept half for operating expenses and decided to use half for the purchase of one cab. A friend told him about leverage and showed him how to use it. He showed Tom how he could buy five cabs with $1,000 down on each.

Tom now operates American Cab Company and EconoRents Car Rental Agency. Three of his cars are cabs and two are used for rentals and back-up taxis. Tom's salary is over $38,000 a year and climbing—because he used the power of leverage even though he didn't need to.

How to Make Big Decisions

Major decisions that can win or lose thousands of dollars must be made, not made for you. Many otherwise creative entrepreneurs put off major decisions, because they are afraid of making the wrong decision. Instead, the decision is made by time. Don't let big decisions give you ulcers. Take advantage of opportunities that require major decisions by doing these things:

- *Break big decisions into smaller decisions.* "Should I expand my business?" can be broken into: "Would an expansion be profitable?," "Would an expansion bring me more business?," "Could I serve my present customers as well if I expanded?," "Can I afford the costs of expansion?" and "Will I be better off a year from now if I expand my business today?"

- *Use a Pro/Con Sheet.* Make two columns on a sheet of paper and label the columns "Pro" and "Con." Write your major decision to be made at the top of the page. Then, list the reasons for and against the decision. Be specific. Your decision will be much easier as you visualize the reasons for and against it.

- *Make a decision!* Whether you take action or not you have made a decision. If you take *no action* on your big decision, it's as if you decided against it. Too often, procrastination is a big decision-maker. So, look at the reasons for and against, and make a clear decision—or time will do it for you.

Big decisions are easier to make when you break them into smaller decisions; use the Pro/Con Sheet you have made and act on the decision you make.

HOW TO REACH YOUR FINAL WEALTH GOAL

You're nearly there. You started by deciding what your long-range financial goal was going to be and how long you expected to take to reach it. Then, you broke your long-range goal into short-range goals and started working on them. You took the first few steps.

Now, you're nearing your journey's end; you're nearing your wealth goal. How are you going to insure yourself that you will reach your goal on time? By taking inventory of your goals and your successes and by making more accurate projections as you near your goal, you will insure a timely success.

If you have followed the suggestions of this book, your goal is earning over $50,000 a year from a home-operated enterprise within the next few years. This is your long-range goal.

The short-range goals of each reader are going to be different. Some expect to reach their financial goal within two years, others within three, five or even ten years. Some will set stepping stones by doubling their income each year until they reach their goal. Others have made plans to add $5,000 or $10,000 to their income each year.

The best method of insuring your success as you reach toward your long-range goal is to evaluate your goal and your successes every few months to keep yourself on track. Ask yourself:

- Is my goal still a good and realistic one?
- Have I set up a timetable for reaching my wealth goal?
- Are my short-range goals explicit enough to show a direct path between where I am now and where I want to be?
- Have I set a realistic timetable for reaching my short-range goals?
- Do my goals need to be modified to insure my success?
- Am I procrastinating? Am I putting off important decisions?

After you've looked ahead and evaluated your goals you should also review the short-range goals you've set and reached. Ask yourself:

- Which short-range goals have succeeded thus far?
- Which ones have failed?
- Is there an obvious reason why some short-range goals have been reached and others have not?
- What short-range goals can I modify to help me complete them and reach my long-range wealth goal sooner?

You've reviewed the course you planned to take as well as the course you are actually taking toward your own wealth goal. By comparing the two and making changes in your road to success as you move along, you can insure that you will reach your goal on time. Ask yourself:

- Overall, how am I doing at moving toward my wealth goal?
- If I follow my present course, can I expect to reach my goal on time?
- What changes in my path can I make to help reach my financial goal?
- Are there short-range goals that I can see as more important or less important than I saw them when I started?
- What can I do to change their importance in my wealth plan?
- What can I do right now to help insure my success in reaching my wealth goal on time?

The Last Mile

The Power of Profit Motivation can take you the last mile to your goal of wealth and independence. Whether you plan to reach that last mile tomorrow, next month, next year or even three years from now, keep the Power of PM in mind and remember how it can help you over the times when you feel you might not reach your goals.

When you feel yourself getting discouraged or low in creative energy, use the Power of Profit Motivation to lift you up by doing these things:

- Completely relax.
- Remind yourself of your final goal.

- Imagine yourself enjoying the benefits of your goal.
- Remind yourself that you have the Power within you to bring these things about.

You can use the Power of Profit Motivation to think your way to success—from the first decision to the last mile. You can remind yourself of the worth of your goals and let your subconscious powers help you convince your mind that you can easily complete them.

You can also use the Power of Profit Motivation to help you solve problems that seem to block the way of your success.

You can use the Power of Profit Motivation right now to help you complete your wealth plan and reach your goal of earning over $50,000 a year at home.

HOW TO SET NEW WEALTH GOALS

You have arrived. You've reached your Profit-Motivated goal of earning $50,000 a year at home. Now what?

During your climb toward financial independence, you learned a lot about business, high-risk ventures, financing opportunities, working with people, advertising and promotion, selecting profitable ventures, developing creative ideas. managing employees, customers and suppliers, distribution and marketing, purchasing and other valuable business skills.

It's time to revise your Skills Worksheet to reflect the entrepreneur you have become. Take a blank sheet of paper and list the skills you have acquired since you took your first step toward your wealth goal. Here are a few idea starters:

- Ability to objectively judge opportunities.
- Competence at using leverage to finance high-risk ventures.
- Knowledge of expert methods of buying and selling.
- Proficiency at building creative ideas into profitable ventures.
- Capability to research and market a wealth venture.

- Working knowledge of record-keeping and profit-accounting.
- Knack for satisfying customers.
- Skill of promoting a wealth venture for higher profits.

These skills and talents, acquired as you climb the ladder of success, are the skills necessary for any entrepreneur to succeed. You've learned the basics of how to turn an idea into profit. You can use these skills in hundreds of potentially profitable situations to continue building your own wealth and worth.

Looking back to your New Skills Worksheet, what skills have you learned that you could modify or improve to bring you even more success?

- Can you easily spot a profitable opportunity?
- Are you knowledgeable enough about accounting to allow you to make the best tax decisions?
- Do you always get along with customers and suppliers?
- Are there areas of financial knowledge that you could improve?
- Have you learned the best and easiest ways to promote your business venture for profit?
- Do you benefit in nearly every bartering encounter?
- Would a better working knowledge of distribution and sales help you earn a higher profit?
- Could you improve your goal-setting methods?

The next question to ask yourself for your New Skills Worksheet is "How can I *improve* my newly developed skills?" Here are a few methods:

- Talk to the most successful people in your trade about their success methods.
- Attend trade shows, seminars and conventions to learn as much as you can about new methods and techniques in your field of opportunities.
- Sign up for a small business administration, financing, supervision or human relations night course at a local school or college.
- Give special thought to the areas where you could improve your skills for higher profits. Study them objectively.

- Read other Parker money-making opportunities books.
- Never stop learning.

Finally, ask yourself what lessons you've learned about Profit Motivation and Success. Start a notebook labeled "Lessons In Success" and write some of your best ideas in it. Keep your notebook nearby and write in it as you read and think of success.

Here are a few idea-starters for your "Lessons in Success":

Profit Motivation is the ambition for personal wealth strong enough to move you to do what is necessary to gain it.

The Power of Profit Motivation is the power of the conscious and subconscious minds to clarify and act on well-defined problems and goals, because they have been motivated to do so with a positive end result.

Set your goal, organize your search, locate the right opportunity then develop your opportunity into riches: these are the steps to GOLD.

The Power of Dollar Dynamics is the power of the dollar to bring you more dollars.

Ramsey's Law: One goal at a time, one step at a time, equals SUCCESS.

You can come up with other lessons you've learned about operating a wealth venture at home and keep them on paper where they can be found years from now and reused.

To repeat the success you've had, you must use all of the skills you've learned—and develop new ones.

How to Write Your New Wealth Goal

Armed with your New Skills Worksheet, you can now write your new wealth goal and feel confident that you will reach it, just as you reached your first one.

Your needs and tastes have changed since you first set your wealth goal back in the early chapters of this book.

What was a luxury might now be a necessity. Your costs and manner of living have changed. You want more out of life now. You've tasted what the Power of Profit Motivation can do to your life, and you don't want to stand still—you want *more*.

This is healthy. Your thirst for the challenge of building new opportunities into a self-satisfying success should be applauded. This drive will not only benefit your life and the lives of those you love, but will also benefit others who directly or indirectly touch your life: storekeepers, investors, employees, suppliers, government officials, recreation businesses, service industries and hundreds of others. The wealth you create for yourself and your business generates opportunity for wealth for others.

How much should your new wealth goal be? It can be as much as you wish to make it. You are an entrepreneur. You are successful at making goals into realities, so you can write almost any goal you wish and assure yourself that you will reach it. You set your first goal at earning over $50,000 a year from a home-operated business. You've reached it. Your new wealth goal could be anything from $100,000 a year to an equity of $1,000,000. You must set your own wealth goal because aiming is the first step to hitting a target.

How to Reach Your New Wealth Goal

Reaching your new wealth goal is going to be much like planning your first wealth goal of $50,000 a year at home. You can reach it with my formula for **GOLD:**

- Set your GOAL.
- ORGANIZE your search.
- LOCATE the right opportunity.
- DEVELOP that opportunity into profits.

In Chapter 1, you read about Byron A. who set his own personal wealth goal at $60,000 within six years. He organized his search for a high-profit skill he could develop or acquire and located the right opportunity, a pick-up canopy manufacturing company operated from his garage. He then developed his wealth plan into a thriving business that doubled his salary every two years. Byron made his $60,000 a year goal almost a year early and began to plan his new wealth goal.

Using the **GOLD** Formula again, Byron set a goal of retiring on a salary of $30,000 a year within five years. He organized his search for the right method of reaching this seemingly impossible goal, but with the help of a business consultant, he came up with the right method. Byron was to build his business to a worth of $300,000, then sell it on a contract at 10 percent interest for 30 years. Byron estimated that his salary as a "consultant" that business would pay his income taxes and give him a salary from the contract of $2,500 free-and-clear each month.

This year, Byron's travel trailer manufacturing firm is reportedly worth $250,000 and Byron is just one short year away from retiring—at the age of 41—on an annual income of $30,000.

The first step toward reaching your new wealth goal is to break it down into easier-to-reach short-range goals. As an example, if your new wealth goal is to raise your earnings from $50,000 to $100,000 a year within four years you can set your short-range goals like this.

First year	$62,500
Second year	$75,000
Third year	$87,500
Fourth year	$100,000

You can then break your first year's goal down even further:

Earn an extra $1,000 to $1,100 each month

To locate the best method of reaching your new wealth goal, look first at your current venture, then to related

ventures and, finally, to completely new enterprises, as outlined in Chapter 8.

Finally, use the Mastermind System, offered in Chapter
6, to develop your new wealth venture toward your new
wealth goal, and you will be on your way to prosperity.

As an idea starter for your second wealth venture, here
is a list of methods used by other entrepreneurs to build their
second fortunes:

- Opening additional outlets for your product or service in other areas.
- Franchising your name and successful methods to others looking for
  wealth.
- Becoming a consultant in your specialized area of wealth.
- Using additional distribution methods (mail, retail outlets, agents,
  franchises).
- Lowering your risk factor by diversifying your business interests.
- Selling your wealth venture with contract terms and beginning a new
  venture in a different field.
- Hiring specialists that you can delegate work to for greater efficiency
  and higher profits.
- Diversifying your investments into the stock market, real estate,
  municipal bonds, syndicates, futures, precious metals, appreciable col-
  lectibles and other opportunities.

You have seen the Power within you that can help you
earn over $50,000 a year from your own home or any other
place you choose. It's the Power of Profit Motivation. The
Power has opened your mind and your life to new ideas—
ideas that have taken you from where you were to a new
world of wealth and prosperity beyond your former dreams.
Use the Power. Make it a part of your life and you can reach
any goal you set for yourself—including the goal of fabulous
wealth.

THINGS YOU CAN DO NOW

You can get your full share of success by using the principles of Success Planning and the Power of Profit

Motivation. To help you reach your new wealth goal—and go beyond it—do these things *right now*:

1. Continue building your current wealth goal with the methods and formulas outlined in this book: the GOLD Formula, the Mastermind System, the Power of Profit Motivation, the Two-Pocket Formula, Dollar Dynamics and others.

2. Check yourself right now to make sure you are following the short-range steps you've set up to insure that you will reach your wealth goal on time. If necessary, make adjustments in your schedule to insure your success over the last mile.

3. Decide on your new wealth goal. Set a new target for your success energies as soon as you reach your first wealth goal. Analyze your new abilities and knowledge and use them to help you build your second fortune.

4. Use the GOLD Formula and Power of Profit Motivation to help you build your second fortune and reach your new wealth goal.

5. Think Profit Motivation.

11

Making
Your Fortune
at Home

The Power of Profit Motivation has given you the power to earn your fortune anywhere you choose: in a luxurious home, in a vacation retreat, aboard a houseboat or yacht, in your own office building—anywhere in the world. It's really up to you.

This chapter offers dozens of methods and ideas for starting and operating your own highly profitable wealth venture from any location you select. The principles will work whether your office is in a large motorhome or a two-story Colonial. The suggestions revolve around a typical home, but can be easily adapted to any type of shelter—by someone as creative as an entrepreneur.

There are many reasons why your home is the best place
for the "home office" of your wealth venture. They include:

- Time efficiency.
- Low overhead.
- Convenience.
- Family involvement.
- Flexible working hours.

The day you move your office to your home is the day
your commuting blues are gone. There is no more fighting
traffic for upwards of an hour, no more high gasoline bills or
train/bus tickets. You can step from your living quarters to
your business doorstep in seconds. You can "go home for
lunch" and enjoy a warm, home-cooked meal with family
and friends. You can knock off early or work a little late.
Your time is used more efficiently for the business of
profits—and the business of living.

Your home-operated business will offer you another
major benefit, a better home. Your business enterprise will
take up 10 to 50 percent of your living area—and can share
the costs of mortgage, utilities, furnishings and
maintenance. You will be able to get tax credit for using part
of your home as your home office, and you will, therefore, be
able to afford a larger and more expensive home.

A home-operated enterprise will allow you to involve
your whole family. You can hire your wife as your secretary
or your husband as your labor force and your children as
mail-room attendants. You can pay them any wage that is
profitable for your new business. If profits are low, you can
cut salaries. If profits are high, you can pass out bonuses.
You can get the whole family involved and working together
on the same satisfying goal.

Another advantage is one that's especially important to
"early birds" and "night owls"—those who prefer to work
while others are resting. A home-operated wealth venture

can often be worked to fit any hours you choose. If your "biological clock" makes you sharper in the mornings, you can choose early office hours and get your work for the day out of the way. The same adaptability of hours is available for late-risers—as long as their enterprise is a flexible one. Your wealth venture could let you work three ' 2-hour days, then have three days off.

An entrepreneur is not tied to a clock—or a location—for his wealth.

YOUR WORK-AT-HOME CHECKLIST

To find out whether you could operate your own wealth venture from your home or other location, ask yourself these questions:

- Do you have a place in your home that could be converted to an adequate and private office?
- Are you a good planner and goal setter? Can you make priority lists and stick to them?
- Would your home office intrude on your family life—or bring it closer together?
- Are you a self-starter? Can you make yourself do the things you need to do?
- Will your family help you with your enterprise? Will they support you? Will they share in the work if needed?
- Will your family cooperate in giving you privacy when you need it?
- Would you enjoy working *and* living in the same house, day after day?

This checklist, answered with your home and family in mind, could point the way to an enjoyable life with a full or part-time enterprise operated from the comfort of your own home.

Where to Set Up Your Home Office

A friend of mine operates an international import and export business from a desk in the corner of his huge master bedroom. Tacked on the wall above his expansive desk is a hand-lettered sign, "Global Trading Company. World Headquarters." The sign may seem out of place to a visitor, but my friend buys and sells over $3 million in merchandise a year from his bedroom suite—more than many downtown office traders.

The point is: Many wealth ventures don't need fancy offices to make huge profits—all they need is an entrepreneur with imagination.

Another entrepreneur, Howard F., started his coin collector's bookstore in an extra bedroom (see Chapter 7). The F.'s had only one child and a three bedroom home so he decided to use the extra room as the "world headquarters" of his company. The part-time venture became full-time, and within two years, the F.'s were forced to buy a large four-bedroom home to keep up with their growing business.

Other wealth builders have started their home-operated business on dining room tables. This is a good short-term location, but as soon as your enterprise needs files, a typewriter and equipment, you may find your family taking a democratic vote for evicting you from your office. If your enterprise is now operating from a dining room table, anticipate your family and move as soon as you can find better quarters.

Businesses that require a workbench or larger equipment are often set up in garages—either in one bay of a double garage or in the rear of a large garage. Expanding enterprises may even take over the whole garage until a larger home is found.

Entrepreneurs have also set up their home offices in:

- Large closets or pantries (one printing broker began with a small desk in a walk-in closet).
- Unfinished room, loft or attic (my office is in the attic of our Cape Cod style home).
- Outbuilding (other entrepreneurs have started in sheds, storage buildings, cabins, converted barns and mother-in-law houses).

- Recreational vehicles (offices can be set up in travel trailers, motor homes and campers that are parked for the season).

Before you set your office up in your home, check with local authorities on zoning requirements, parking areas and permits needed for signs.

HOW TO SET UP YOUR HOME OFFICE

It's time to choose the location for your home office and start setting it up in anticipation of the day you can work in it full time. Your home office may need to be more than just an office. Your wealth venture may need a shipping area, a work area and an equipment and manufacturing area. To choose the best location in your home for your home office, keep your enterprise's needs in mind as you ask these questions:

- Do I need a paperwork area? How large? Will I need a typewriter? Files? A desk?
- Will my enterprise require a manufacturing or working area? How large? What equipment will I need in it? How can I best lay out the equipment for efficiency?
- Do I need a distribution or shipping area? If so, will my paperwork area be sufficient? Will I need special mailing equipment? Do I need extra warehouse space for my product?

Then, look at your present home and its available space as you ask yourself:

- What is the total number of square feet that I will need for my enterprise?
- What are the three best locations in my home for my new enterprise?
- Which is the *best* location for my venture?

As you decide on the location of your home office, keep in mind your venture's requirements, your home's limitations, the possibility of expansion and your family's and customers' needs.

Answering these questions will also help you decide on the equipment you'll need for your enterprise. Most, if not all, wealth ventures will have one piece of equipment in common: a typewriter. Your typewriter need not be fancy, but the keys must be clean and readable—and it should be easy to use. You'll be using it to type letters to customers and suppliers, keep records of your business, prepare shipping labels and dozens of other jobs. You can buy a typewriter new or used, rent it, or even borrow it—but you must have one.

Each new enterprise will require different equipment. Make a complete list of the equipment your wealth venture will need, then plan how you are going to purchase or lease it. Your list could include:

Typewriter	Band saw
File cabinet	Sewing machine
Desk	Collator
Chair(s)	Sander/grinder
Work bench	Drills
Postage meter	Painting equipment
Copy machine	Commercial oven
Scales	Envelope stuffer
Hand tools	Mimeograph
Radial saw	Cash register

SET UP YOUR OWN RECORDS FOR PROFIT

For most people, record keeping is the dullest part of operating a wealth venture. But to an entrepreneur, it's the most exciting because it shows him not only *how much* profit he's making, but *where* he's making it—and *how*. A smart entrepreneur will spend a good deal of time reading over the books of his venture, searching for successes that can be enlarged and failures that can be turned around. And your "books" can tell you all of this and more.

You will want two types of books in your enterprise:

- Dollar Inventory.
- Material Inventory.

Your *Dollar Inventory* records will show you where your dollars are coming from, where they are going and what percentages are involved. Your books will be:

- Cash Journals (for recording incoming and outgoing money).
- Ledgers (list of income and expenses by type).
- Statements (balance sheets, profit and loss statements, to list income, expenses and profit).

Your *Material Inventory* will be for businesses making and selling a product. Your books will show:

- Raw Materials (records of what raw materials are on hand and where they came from).
- In Process (records of raw materials being made into products).
- Finished Products (inventory of completed products ready for shipping to customers).

Material inventories not only show you where your raw materials are in the manufacturing process, but also point out losses and inefficiencies and can even suggest ways of correcting them for greater profit.

Such detailed record keeping may seem unnecessary to the average person, but to the entrepreneur, the business records are the pulse of his wealth venture. He knows that more businesses fail because of poor record-keeping than any other cause.

There's another reason for complete records—taxes. As a self-employed person you must now pay taxes directly to the local, state and federal governments, rather than have

your employer do it. The better your records, the easier it is
to earn tax credits and take advantage of tax allowances.

It is not the aim of this book to give you tax advice.
Rather, a smart entrepreneur will equip himself with half a
dozen questions and buy an hour or two of a tax consultant
or accountant's time—it will be very profitable time. A
professional tax person can show you how to legally write off
portions of your home, your car, vacations, investments,
retirement funds, insurance and other necessary expenses to
keep your profits high and your taxes low.

An entrepreneur soon learns this rule: The time to think
about taxes is *before* you have to pay them. Tax planning
may be the most important skill you can add to your Skills
Worksheet. Talk to your tax consultant or accountant.

KNOWLEDGE IS PROFIT

Your profit will be in direct proportion to your
knowledge and your ability to use that knowledge. You have
created a wealth enterprise based on what you know and
what you expect to be able to sell it for. The road to greater
profits continues by increasing your knowledge. That can be
done by starting your Entrepreneur Library right now.

One section of your Entrepreneur Library will be for
books on your trade. If you are selling crafts, you'll want to
start purchasing—and studying—books on those crafts,
similar crafts, how to sell crafts and related topics. If you are
a mechanic, you'll want books on maintenance and repair. If
your enterprise is a workshop venture, you'll want to add
books on making things with wood and metal. If your
venture is service oriented, you'll want books about your
field and how to service your customers.

Another section of your new library will include books
on "entrepreneurship"—and the book you're holding can

be the first. Other Parker Publishing books on money-making opportunities include:

Big Time Opportunities and Strategies That Turn Pennies into Millions by Forrest H. Frantz, Sr.

The Complete Handbook of How to Start and Run a Money-Making Business in Your Home by Marian Behan Hammer

How to Borrow Everything You Need to Build a Great Personal Fortune by Herbert Holtje and John Stockwell

How to Borrow Your Way to a Great Fortune by Tyler G. Hicks

How to Earn a Fortune and Become Independent in Your Own Business by Merle E. Dowd

How to Make a Quick Fortune: New Ways to Build Wealth Fast by Tyler G. Hicks

How to Start Your Own Business on a Shoestring and Make up to $100,000 a Year by Tyler G. Hicks

Money Making Secrets of the Millionnaires by Hal D. Steward

100 Ways to Make Money in Your Spare Time, Starting with Less Than $100 by John Stockwell and Herbert Holtje

Second Income Money Makers by Scott Witt

Secrets of Top Money Extra Income by Edith L. Johnson

Spare-Time Fortune Guide by Duane G. Newcomb

Knowledge is money. The more wealth-building secrets you learn and apply, the more wealth you can earn. A smart entrepreneur invests a minimum of five percent of his net profits into self-improvement books and courses—to *insure* future successes.

HOW TO OPERATE YOUR HOME OFFICE

You've set up and equipped your home wealth venture—and you're ready to get down to business. As you start your business on a part-time basis and build it to a full-time enterprise, your office hours and priorities for getting things done will change. To decide on the best office hours at any stage of your venture ask yourself these questions:

- Do I have to build my business hours around another job or activity?
- Do I function more productively at one time of day than I do at others? Early morning? Just after lunch? Early evenings? Late nights?
- How many hours per week must I devote to my enterprise to keep it profitable and help it grow?
- Should I operate my venture throughout the week or just one or two days a week?
- What would the best and most productive hours be for my wealth venture?

The most productive way to do the things you need to do is, of course, to work by priorities. Chapter 10 offered methods and examples of using a limited amount of time to take care of the most necessary and profitable duties. They include: (1) Making daily lists of things you need to do, (2) Marking them in order of their priority, (3) Doing them in the order of their priority

Priority is productivity—and productivity is profit.

What to wear? It's easy when you're working with someone else; your bosses and co-workers dictate the clothes you will wear. Professionals will wear a business suit, mechanics will wear coveralls and factory workers will wear sturdy work clothes. But when you are your own boss, you must decide what type of clothing is most appropriate. If you deal with the public, you should probably wear what others in your trade are wearing, not necessarily to conform, but because work clothing should be practical. If you're not dealing with the public—if your home wealth venture is a mail-order publishing firm, a phone sales firm, or similar enterprise—you can choose any kind of clothing you wish to wear from a suit to swim trunks. You can wear whatever best fits your lifestyle.

HOW TO HANDLE THE HIRED HELP

Do you need help to operate your enterprise? Who should you hire—and why? As the operator of a home-based business you probably have a built-in workforce: spouse, children, friends and neighbors. How much you should rely on this close workforce depends on your business needs, your pocketbook and your closeness to family and friends.

The first step toward building your work force is to define the job or jobs you need done. Do you need someone to type letters for you? Someone to assemble parts? Someone to keep your books? Someone to deliver merchandise? What would their duties be? How many hours per day, week or month would you need them? Could you combine two or three jobs for one employee? How much can you pay for each task and still keep your operation profitable?

Next, you should look at your available work force for people with the skills you need. Does your wife type or keep books? Can your husband handle deliveries and distribution? Are your children capable of assembling your product without error? Keep in mind that it's often better to get family members involved in your wealth venture if you can, but your highest priority must be to make it a profitable business that hires efficient employees who can do the jobs necessary at a reasonable cost to you. Your first duty to your family is to earn a good living. If you can involve them in your wealth venture and make the family a tighter unit, all the better.

Whether or not your family is involved in your profitable enterprise, there are certain rules you will have to set up for yourself and for them, so that you all can enjoy the benefits of having a business at home.

Once you've set up your venture you'll want to have an understanding with family members about the operation of your business. Your spouse and children should understand the basics of your home wealth venture and should respect your need for privacy. One home businessman I know uses an extra bedroom for his phone-oriented business. Bert's wife and children understand that when the door to his office is open, they can come in to talk about family things. They also understand that when his office door is closed, he is in business and only business messages should be relayed. If they must answer his phone they answer, "Phoenix Enterprises," rather than just "Hello." They know that when Bert comes out of his room, "Daddy is home from work" and can play—or take out the garbage.

A disadvantage of home-operated wealth ventures is having to spend most of your 24 hours under the same roof. Smart entrepreneurs know that the boredom of being in the same place for too long decreases efficiency. They also know how to combat it. Many of them spend part of the year—or even part of the week or month—in their second office, a vacation retreat. The owner of Phoenix Enterprises got his firm name from his second home in Phoenix, Arizona. His main office is in Portland, Oregon, and he spends the spring and summer there. The fall and winter are spent in a chalet-style home just outside of Phoenix. Portions of the cost of both homes are tax deductible.

The point is, your home-operated wealth venture offers you the freedom of making your fortune anywhere you choose. Take advantage of this independence. Get away—and take your business with you.

HOW TO HANDLE THE PHONE AND MAIL

A talk with a phone company representative will give you ideas for profitably using your telephone. Depending upon your needs, you can get phones with two or more lines, hold buttons, automatic call transfer, automatic dialing systems, paging units and other inventions, to help to get down to the business of making money easier.

One of the best investments for the one-person office is an answering service or answering machine. An answering service—which is probably run by another entrepreneur—can take your calls while you're out or away from your desk, forward them to your new location or number or page you with an electronic beeper. Often less expensive, a phone message-recording device, available at many larger stores, will keep you from losing that important call. Take a look at your phone needs. There's probably a gadget or service available to help you make your profit venture more profitable.

Why would anyone want to call you? They call you for help, they want information or they want to order something from you. That's why starting off on the correct foot when you answer your phone is so important. People who call want to hear a friendly voice tell them they got the right number, who they are talking to and a request to assist them. You might answer your phone something like this man does:

"Phoenix Enterprises. This is Bert. May I help you?"

As the phone rings in front of him, Bert takes a deep breath, relaxes and thinks of what he is going to say to the caller in a slow and warm voice. He asks their name as soon as he can and uses it throughout their conversation. Many of Bert's customers never see him, so he tries to give them a picture of a mature, considerate person, who wants very much to please his customers. It works, and Bert earns well over $65,000 a year from his home-operated business.

The mails are the next best communicator. In fact, most home-operated businesses will reach more customers through the mail than they will by phone. That's why it's important to put your best side forward with quality stationery, literature and forms.

If you use the mails for much of your business, here are a few things you should know to earn higher profits:

- There are four classes of mail: *first class* for letters, *second class* for magazines and newspapers, *third class* for books, catalogs and circulars, and *fourth class* for parcels and books. Most businesses use first class for letters and *third class bulk rate* for circulars.

- If you handle much correspondence set up a system of marking incoming envelopes as to whether they are ordering or asking for information. Answer mail with either a form letter or pre-written paragraphs that can be typed fresh for each correspondence. For example, you can ask your secretary to write a letter using paragraphs 1, 9, 14, 3 and 7. It will save both of you time, while giving a personal response rather than a form letter.

- If you prefer not to have customers come to your home, rent a box at a local post office. Or, if you live in a small town, ask the postmaster to allow you to drop your street address from correspondence. Some post offices will permit this.

- Most important, handle your correspondence as you would your phone; be warm and informal. Correspondence that reads: "We beg to call your attention to the enclosed statement" is out. Write as you speak and your customers will understand you. Smile at them on paper and they will like you.

Operating your home office profitably and by priorities can make your wealth venture—and your family life—more enjoyable.

HIGH-PROFIT METHODS FOR THE HOME
WEALTH-BUILDER

Here are six words that can be worth *100 times* the price of this book:

Keep an Idea Notebook with you.

That's right. As you learn to turn ideas into profit, you are going to find yourself getting more and more profitable ideas—at any time of the day or night—and it's difficult to remember them later when you need them. So, buy a small spiral bound notebook that you can carry with you in your pocket or purse, and start writing down these gems as they strike you. You can always go back later and sort them out for profitability and usefulness.

One entrepreneur I know carries his notebook with him all day and sets it by his bed at night. He averages two or three new ideas a day. Most of them are discarded within a week, but a few have gone on to make him money. In fact, some of them have made him over $10,000 each. This smart businessman now owns six businesses operated under two corporations—because he carries and uses an Idea Notebook.

My own Idea Notebook system works like this:

- I carry my notebook constantly and spend 15 minutes of my lunch hour looking it over for idea starters.
- I take the best ideas and transfer them to 3 x 5" index cards, so they can be filed by subject in my Idea File.
- I review my Idea File at least once a week for ideas that can be applied to projects I'm working on that week.
- I file Ideas Being Used in the rear of my file and estimate profit or savings on the back of the card.

Over half of my yearly income can be directly traced back to my Idea Notebook and Idea File. You can accomplish the same thing. You can *double* your income by starting—and using—your own Idea Notebook.

As an entrepreneur you have the power to earn over $50,000 a year from your own home or anywhere else you choose. Use this power wisely, and your life will change dramatically.

THINGS YOU CAN DO NOW

If you haven't already begun to make high profits and enjoy the benefits of wealth at home, do these things *right now:*

1. Set up your home office. Choose the best location. Decide on the equipment and supplies you'll need. Begin your record-keeping system. Build your wealth-building library.

2. Plan your home office hours and decide whether you need to hire additional help to run your venture. Consider your family for employees. Learn to use the phone and mails for profit.

3. Start your Idea Notebook. Begin building a more profitable future with ideas. Review your Idea Notebook at least once a week to find new applications for your ideas. Turn your best ideas into greater profits.

4. Think Profit Motivation.

12

Six Powerful Ways
to Make—And Keep—
More MONEY

Lou H.—a man who started with nothing and built a fortune of nearly $2 million in less than 10 years—gave me some profitable counsel: *Making* money is the easy part, it's *keeping* it that's hard.

He's right.

Once you've built your own fortune through the Power of Profit Motivation you'll find that the biggest problem you have is keeping your fortune from the tax man, who can legally take *half or more* of your riches. Inflation will also take part of your fortune.

The final chapter in this book is about how you can *make even more* than $50,000 a year at home—and how to legally *keep more of what you make*.

WHAT IS MONEY?

Let's start at the beginning. Money is

* A medium of exchange.
* A measure of value.

With money comes power. It can be a power for good or a power for bad. Money can bring you all of the things you've ever wanted: a larger home, finer cars, an education, travel and peace of mind. Or, money can bring you all of the things you never wanted: problems, worry, distrust and insecurity. It all depends on how you use your money—your power. I sincerely hope that the power you've learned about in this book will bring you not just money, but will bring you the happiness, prosperity and self-fulfillment that money can offer.

You've heard it said: Money isn't everything—but it's an excellent way of keeping score. That's a fact. You are going to be paid by other people based on the amount of service you give to them. Small wages mean little service. A vast fortune means you are giving others something they need very much—something they need more than the money they give you. So money is an excellent way of keeping score of your success at serving others.

Money is Good!

Money will bring you your basic needs: food, clothing, shelter and transportation. You can provide most of these things for yourself and your family without money, but money is an efficient medium of exchange that can give you more than you could do yourself. Two hundred years ago, it took most of a person's waking hours to provide adequate food, shelter and other basic needs. Today, you have the potential of earning enough of our efficient exchange, money, to satisfy your living needs with just a few hours work each day.

Money can then fulfill your hopes and dreams. The Power of Money can bring you a more comfortable and worry-free life. Money can help you enjoy your life with not only more free hours, but also with a medium of exchange that will bring you things that will help you enjoy these extra hours. Today, the Power of Money can take you to places never seen by the greatest explorers of just a few hundred years ago. The Power of Money can bring you gadgets, contraptions and playthings unavailable even to the super-rich of just a few decades ago. The Power of Money *can* buy you happiness and a better life.

MAKING IT—AND KEEPING IT

Our efficient economy also takes its dues from those who earn more money. The tax man's rule is: The more you earn, the more you can afford to pay. Under present IRS laws, people making $50,000 a year are in the "50 percent tax bracket." This means that anything they earn over $50,000 is taxed at the rate of 50%—unless they can find legal tax loopholes that exempt part or all of this extra income.

This tax rule sounds discouraging to the entrepreneur. Once he achieves a comfortable living, why should he earn *more* money knowing that *half* of it will go to Uncle Sam? Because the smart entrepreneur understands how to use the "unless," and he can find legal tax loopholes that exempt part, or all, of this extra income. The smart entrepreneur sees that the best investment he can make is in expert tax counsel. He knows that these perfectly legal exemptions in our tax laws can allow him to charge off his home office expenses, part of his car expenses, some of his travel expenses and entertainment expenses—even portions of his income—before counting out the tax man's share.

The smart entrepreneur also understands that our efficient economy is much like walking up a down escalator: If you stand still you are losing ground. An investor is always concerned with the present value of future dollars. As an example, with a 6 percent per year inflation rate, a promise to pay you $100 in 5 years is only worth $74.73 today. A promise of $100 in 20 years is only worth $31.18 of today's dollars. So, your dollars have to *grow* just to keep up.

The tax man and inflation—those are the problems of making money. Here are my six methods for making and keeping money:

Power #1—The Power of PM.

Power #2—Power to Learn, Grow and Profit.

Power #3—Power of **GOLD**.

Power #4—Power of Money Control.

Power #5—Power of Tax Knowledge.

Power #6—Power of Second Fortune Motivation.

Power #1

Earl Nightingale is a motivator. He makes his living by speaking to others—on records, on tapes and at conventions—about motivation. One of his most quoted proverbs is:

Anything the mind of man can conceive and believe it can achieve.

What he's saying is: To reach anything you want, you must first *see* it in your mind, then *believe* you can reach it. This concept is part of the Power of Profit Motivation. The Power of PM goes farther and shows you how to place your needs and your desires within your subconscious. The Power of PM can be used to set up life goals, short-term goals, solve both large and small problems, find profitable wealth ventures and develop them into enterprises that can offer you over $50,000 a year at home—or any other goal you set for yourself.

Let's review the steps to using the Power of Profit Motivation:

- Find a completely quiet place to relax. Sit back in a comfortable chair and let your daily problems vanish for a few moments. Don't worry about anything. Turn out the lights and become aware of your mind. Completely turn off your physical senses.

- Study your problem or develop your goal. If you are trying to solve a problem, look at the problem as your best friend or business associate would. Break your problem down into smaller problems that can be more easily conquered. In your mind, list some of the possible solutions. If you are trying to develop a short- or long term goal, imagine yourself reaching that goal. If your goal is earning $50,000 at home, see yourself working in your home office, then spending your impressive salary on cars, boats, planes, vacations or any other dreams.

- Tell yourself, "I have the Power within me right now to earn riches and find happiness in such great abundance that I can easily share both with others." Repeat it. Keep this sentence on a small card with you in your pocket or purse. Remind yourself that you have the Power to make it come true.

The Power of Profit Motivation is within you right now. The Power of Profit Motivation is the power of the conscious and subconscious minds to clarify and act on well-defined problems and goals because they have been motivated to do so with a positive end result. The Power of Profit Motivation offers more than just monetary profit—it also brings you the profit of growth. The Power of PM can also help you get more out of life than others. The Power of Profit Motivation can bring you riches beyond your dreams.

Power #2

The second power you'll use to make and keep more money is the *Power to Learn, Grow and Profit.* As you use the Power of PM to develop your own wealth goals and build your profitable enterprise, you'll be learning, growing and profiting from the situations you conquer with PM. You'll learn how to make the best of the most valuable things around you including:

- Yourself.
- Your money.
- Your skills.
- Your surroundings.
- Your family.
- Your life.

The Power of Profit Motivation will breed this second power, the Power to Learn, Grow and Profit, and this second power will give birth to others. It never stops. As you find the power within you to solve any problem that arises, you will find the Power of Self-Confidence. As you find the power to develop profit from almost any worthwhile venture, you will discover the Power of Entrepreneurship. As you find the power within you to become an expert on any subject you wish, you will discover the Power of the Mind. All these powers are combined in the Power to Learn, Grow and Profit—a power that you have *right now*.

Power #3

Your third power is the *Power of* GOLD. As you remember from earlier chapters, it's the Power to :

- Set your **GOALS**.
- **ORGANIZE** your search.
- **LOCATE** the right opportunity.
- **DEVELOP** your opportunities into riches.

The Power of GOLD can help you set your long- and short-range goals. It can help you decide on your final wealth goal—and show you how to develop it to reality.

The Power of GOLD—used with the Power of Profit Motivation—will help you set your goal as a believable and obtainable figure that you feel will bring you more happiness and enjoyment from life. It can be any goal you wish: $25,000, $50,000, $100,000 or more a year; a lump sum figure like $500,000, $1,000,000 or more; or a specific number of businesses, cars, houses, boats or any other easily countable goal.

The Power of **GOLD** will then help you organize your search for the best method of reaching that goal. The Power will show you how to find and analyze your current skills, then show you how to develop the skills you will need to reach your goal. The Power will break your long-range wealth goal into smaller, easier-to-reach goals that can assure you of success.

The Power of **GOLD** can help you locate the right opportunity to help you reach your wealth goal by showing you how to use another power—the Power of Dollar Dynamics—to make your dollars earn more dollars. The power of **GOLD** will show you how to count your resources, look for opportunity everywhere, estimate the potential of each opportunity with Ramsey's Opportunity Ratio and, finally, choose the most Dollar Dynamic opportunity.

The fourth step in using the Power of **GOLD**, developing your opportunities into riches, uses the Mastermind System to research and develop your wealth-building opportunities into full-fledged wealth ventures. It takes you the final mile to reaching your financial goal.

As you set your wealth goals remember to:

- Be specific.
- Be realistic.
- Make them attainable.
- Make them desirable.
- Make them believable.
- Make them measurable.
- Make them challenging.
- List them by priority.
- Set specific completion dates.

Also remember that goals are set to motivate you to reach them. If your goals seem too far off, it's more difficult to see your success of reaching that goal. Break your major goals into smaller easier-to-reach ones. If your goal is to earn over $50,000 a year at home within four years and you're earning $10,000 a year now, the logical step is to set goals of earning $10,000 more this year than you did last year. Rather than jump from $10,000 a year to $50,000 a year, you are stepping from $10,000 to $20,000 to $30,000 to $40,000 and finally to your goal of $50,000 a year.

Power #4

The next power you will use to make and keep more money is the Power of Money Control. It's the Power to keep tight controls on the money that passes through your enterprise. This Power is built by:

- Controlling income.
- Controlling expenses.
- Controlling cash flow.
- Controlling customers.
- Controlling employees.

As an entrepreneur—a business builder—you will soon learn the magic ratio of effort-to-profit for your new wealth venture. You'll see a direct relationship between the amount of work you do, or have done for you, and the amount of business it brings. You will see how much effort it takes to sell one hour of service, one used car, one wooden windmill, one ceramic lamp, or one anything-else-you're-selling. This ratio of effort-to-profit is the key to controlling your income. If you can find this ratio you can increase and decrease your wealth venture's income and thus control your profit. Controlling income is the first step to earning and keeping higher profits.

As you decide at what level to price your product or service, you will list and analyze the expenses you expect to have to pay in order to produce it. You should be able to come up with a cost per unit. Then, you set your retail price based on your expenses *plus* the profit you want to earn per unit. You know that if you want to keep the same amount of profit with the same retail price you must also keep your expenses at a constant level. This is Expense Control and it is critical to your profit picture.

You can control expenses by:

- Setting up income, expense and profit ratios per unit.
- Keeping adequate records.

This leads us to the third part of the Power of Money Control, controlling cash flow. Cash flow is the number of dollars going in and out of your business. By setting up a cash-flow ratio you can profit with the principle of cash turnover. It works like the following example.

If your records tell you that the cash flow for your business is about $100,000 a year and your cash-flow-to-profit ratio is 10:1 you can see that your profit is about $10,000. Using this cash-flow ratio you can also see that if you were to increase your cash flow—the money moving in and out of your business—to $500,000, your profit would be about $50,000. You can easily control your cash flow by setting up a cash-flow-to-profit ratio and then increasing the amount of dollars running through your business.

The fourth way of controlling money in your wealth venture is to control your customers. You must:

- *Learn how to turn them on.* Learn how to control their buying with the Powers of Dollar Dynamics and Profit Motivation. Learn how to help them buy from you by watching them closely for their *buying motives.* Help them buy with easy credit and encourage them to pay your bill with discounts. Control your customers.

- *Learn how to turn them off.* It sounds crazy, but there will be times when you will want to slow your business down for short periods of time. You may reach a point where you will have to expand into larger quarters and a larger cost if you get any more customers. You may wish to sell just a certain amount of units to retain quality control. You may want to take a well-deserved vacation and curtail your business for a few days, weeks or months. Watch your customers' *buying motives* and you will learn how to tactfully defer business during times you don't want or need it and insure that they will come back when you do.

Finally, to build the Power of Money Control you must learn how to control your largest expense—employees. In most businesses, the biggest number of dollars that comes in is sent right back out the door with employees. Many businesses expect salaries and employee-related expenses to top 50% of their income.

Keep your employees loyal. Help them understand their part of your enterprise and how they are contributing to the whole. Show them how they can rise within your business to earn more money and more prestige. Treat your employees as you would your family, and they will become a second family to you—loyal, helpful, considerate.

Power #5

The fifth power to help you make and keep more money is the Power of Tax Knowledge. An old adage says, "The only things for certain are death and taxes." I think man will probably overcome death before he rids himself of the burden of taxes. Our tax structure is not based on a certain percent of what we make. Rather it is a sliding scale tax structure based on a thousand variables subject to twice as many interpretations.

Taxes were covered in part in Chapter 11. What I would like to stress is that the best investment you can make as you climb your ladder of success is an investment in expert tax advice. The average citizen starts planning his taxes on April 14. The smart entrepreneur begins planning his taxes on

January 1. He knows that a few smart tax decisions can make the difference between success and failure.

The smart entrepreneur also knows that a tax consultant or certified public accountant is trained and bonded to give him expert advice on how to buy and sell property, how and where to invest profits, how to cope with profit and loss, how to depreciate capital assets, how to double his profit without doubling his income, and can provide him with other worthwhile information. Expert tax advice is often worth ten or more times its price.

Power #6

The final—and most important—Power you will need to help you earn and keep more money is the Power of Second Fortune Motivation. Chapter 5 introduced you to the Power of Dollar Dynamics, the power of the dollar to bring you more dollars. Chapter Eight showed you how to use leverage in building your empire and how to diversify your interests for ever greater and more secure profits. You can use both of these powers to build your second fortune quickly.

You've set your goals on financial independence and security. You've seen the Power of Profit Motivation and the related powers at work. You realize that your second fortune will be much easier to build than your first—except for one thing, motivation. When you started building your financial future with this book, you quickly realized that you were underpaying yourself. You saw that there was much you were missing in life. You were Profit-Motivated to begin on your way to wealth. If you've used the Powers as suggested in this book, you have probably secured much of the wealth you were searching for, and some of your profit motivation is gone. Here's what to do to insure success for your second fortune:

Motivate yourself with another kind of profit.

That's right. You can motivate yourself to build your second fortune with another—even more important—profit. It's the Profit of Living. Once you've satisified the financial needs of yourself and your family, and you've reached the point in your life where you have confidence in your own ability to be a success, you will do one of two things:

1. Retire for life

   or

2. Search for more challenges.

The theme of this book involves more than the earning of over $50,000 income each year from any location you wish. The theme is how to find enjoyment in life without selling your life away. Hundreds of thousands—even millions—of people sell themselves short. They give no more consideration to their career and plan for life than they would to choosing a new coat. They plod from day to day with no energy, no enthusiasm and no motivation.

But, you have learned the secrets of successful living. You have learned how to profit—financially *and* in life. You have learned not only how to earn more money than most of your friends and relatives, but also—and nearly as important—how to serve others and be of greater value to their lives.

That's what I mean when I say that you can insure success for your second fortune by motivating yourself with another kind of profit. The profit formula as applied to life would read something like this:

Your assets (talents, ability, knowledge) minus your liabilities (what you haven't paid back) equals your net worth or net profit.

Your second fortune will not be built from a need for financial wealth, but from a need to gain the respect and good feelings of yourself and others. The money will come with it, and you will have a lifetime of financial security—and something more.

Go for your second fortune.

WHY OTHERS WON'T BE AS WEALTHY AS YOU

Researchers tell us that only about five percent of the people in this nation reach financial *independence* by the age of 65. Only one in 20 has earned enough—and invested enough—during their 47 years of working to be able to not rely on inadequate retirement funds and social security checks for at least part of their existence. Why?

Because they don't know what *you* know.

The other 95 percent doesn't really have the imagination it takes to see the opportunities that are available all around—like fruits on a tree—waiting to be picked and enjoyed.

The other 95 percent doesn't know how to get motivated. These individuals don't understand the Power of Profit Motivation. They don't know of the power within them right now that can change their lives into more profitable lives (in more ways than one).

The other 95 percent doesn't have the drive and determination that comes with setting goals—and sticking with them. They can't see the other end of the rainbow so they don't even try to imagine it. They don't know how to take that first step into a profitable future.

You know. *You* understand. *You* have the imagination, motivation and determination it takes to reach out for the stars and grasp them. That's why you are worth more. That's why you can earn over $50,000 a year at home—you have the power within you right now to earn twice that much.

Think Profit Motivation.

THINGS YOU CAN DO NOW

You have the power within you *right now* to make—and keep—more money. Do these things:

1. Understand money. Money is a medium of exchange and a measure of value. Money is an excellent way of keeping track of your success at serving others.

2. Learn how to keep more of the money you make. Use the Power of Profit Motivation. Learn, grow and profit. Use the Power of setting goals. Learn the Power of Money Control, the Power of Tax Knowledge, and the Power of Your Second Fortune.

3. Decide that you are not going to be among the 95 percent of retirees without financial independence. Decide *right now* that you are going to be among the other 5 percent who can enjoy the rest of your life in financial security.

4. If you haven't done so—or if you need a fresh start—start toward your goal of earning over $50,000 a year at home *right now*.

5. Think Profit Motivation.

Index